D0708025

LOOKING IN JUNK SHOPS

Also by John Bedford

MORE LOOKING IN JUNK SHOPS

TALKING ABOUT TEAPOTS

THE COLLECTING MAN

LOOKING IN
JUNK SHOPS

JOHN BEDFORD

Illustrations by
Susan Holland

MAX PARRISH · LONDON

MAX PARRISH AND CO LTD
Gulf House
2 Portman Street
W.1

First published in 1961
Ninth impression 1969
SBN 356 01081 3

Made and Printed in Great Britain by
Purnell & Sons Ltd, Paulton (Somerset) and London

Preliminary Chat

Today, more and more people are becoming aware that things made a long time ago can have a special quality not to be found in the wares of their own age. Perhaps the things of today are too near us to have enchantment: possibly our grandchildren will like them better than we do.

But since the war, the prices of many much-collected antiques have soared beyond the reach of ordinary persons. Is there anything left for them to collect? I think there is.

First, a word about this little book. It is the product of browsing about in junk sheds and posh antique shops, of gossiping with dealers and other collectors, of thumbing through books by experts. There are enormous gaps in it, due sometimes to my own ignorance, sometimes to the fact that nothing is as yet known about a subject.

So although the book is arranged in A to Z order, it doesn't set up to be an encyclopaedia. In fact each entry is rather like the window of a junk shop: if you see something that interests you, go inside – to the Reading List at the end of the book, which will direct you to specialists who know all the available facts.

When a word appears in CAPITALS it is supposed to have an entry of its own, so it is usually worth battling on through the large letters. At the end of the book there is a section on marks, together with some cautionary remarks about them.

On the whole this book steers clear of those terrifying places where the carpets are thick and the shelves are lined with Georgian cut-glass and MEISSEN PORCELAIN. A glance *is* given in that direction, for many a collector who starts in the junk shops has ultimately found his way into these establishments. After all, for full enjoyment there is nothing like the best.

But by the time anyone has actually reached these heady regions, either they don't need help at all, or they can turn to the admirable specialist textbooks. What we are much more concerned with here is trying to help the complete beginner; also in taking a closer look at some of the things, not of the much-collected day before yesterday, but of yesterday itself. Many of them are still in the junk shops – but only just. In a few years' time you may have to walk over the thick carpets to buy them.

This doesn't mean that any particular date limit has been set. The United States Customs takes the year 1830 for the dividing line between antiques and non-antiques, as do the annual Antique Dealers' Fairs. But just as there are still some very reasonably priced things from before that date, so there is much Victoriana, or even Edwardiana, whose value is already on the Sotheby level.

Generally speaking, the book does not cover items like match-boxes, postage stamps and shrunken human heads, all of which have their devoted collectors. Here we are more interested, by and large, in things that one keeps for their looks.

If some of these things are astonishing rather than beautiful, it should be remembered that as fashions change, so do our feelings about fashions. The Victorians disliked and even despised those eighteenth-century styles which we now adore: we ourselves are beginning to like much of what the Victorians liked. But presently we may dislike it again and prefer the streamlined things of this century's twenties; we may even nip smartly back into, say, an Edwardian appreciation of Elizabethan oak. The point is that our eyes are, as you might say, changing under our very eyes. What seems at first to be horrible, later becomes interesting, then fascinating. After that you take its beauty for granted.

A word about dealers, who come in astonishing variety. If you want to form a serious collection of properly authenticated pieces in an already collected field and you have the money to do it, go to a member of the British Antique Dealers' Association (whose plaque is usually in the window), and buy from him or get him to buy for you. You may completely rely upon his guarantee.

But if you want some fun and excitement, and perhaps run a few risks, if you prefer to strike out into fields which haven't yet been seriously collected but seem to be worth it, the place for you is the junk shop.

One advantage you have over all dealers is that to make a living they have to turn their money over as quickly as possible, so in the main they have to follow current demands. As a collector, however, you have no need to sell and can consequently buy cheaply by getting out of step with passing fashions, by going for things which other people haven't yet thought of or have lost interest in for the moment.

To do this successfully you will have to rely on your own taste, for there are no connoisseurs to help you; and no doubt as time goes on you may find yourself blushing at the sight of your early purchases. But this is an excellent sign of improving taste, so cull your things remorselessly and buy again.

By what standards? Well, if you go for things of basically sound design (which really only means that they look nice), which preferably – though not necessarily – have some individual craftsmanship about them, and which seem to have been made sincerely either for practical use or to please, then you can't go far wrong.

But collecting, if it is to be anything more than mere accumulating, must be an entirely personal pleasure. So, once again, please yourself: but also *please* yourself. As an old dealer said to me once: 'You know, if you like something, it's surprising how soon you forget what it cost; if you don't like it, the thing's dear at any price!' The most successful collectors have been those who bought neither for investment nor to be in the fashion, nor for personal prestige. They may have started in any of these ways, but they generally ended by buying things because they knew about them and liked them. You could say they bought them for love.

JOHN BEDFORD

A Note with the New Revised Edition

Gratifyingly many people seem to have enjoyed looking over one's shoulder into junk shops during the past three years, and also in writing copiously and interestingly of their own adventures in these Merlin's Caves.

So much so that it seemed to justify offering a second book – *More Looking in Junk Shops* – to cover items crowded out of the first or given scant treatment there.

This second book now goes into a new printing: and I hope that any new friends it makes will not hesitate to push open the door and come into the shop.

J.B.

American Views
If, on turning over a pile of old dinner plates, you
come across any with obviously American views or
subjects, don't use them to give the dog his dinner on.
They have been heavily collected – chiefly by Americans, of course – for many years now, and when they
bob up they make extraordinarily high prices.

But the point is that they *do* bob up occasionally,
for to the innocent eye, like all STAFFORDSHIRE PRINTED
EARTHENWARE, they do simply look like dinner plates.
They were turned out by nearly all the leading potters
and also many hundreds of obscure ones and, naturally enough, went in vast quantities to the United
States. But don't be deceived by modern 'reprints'
made, not with any intention to deceive, but in res-
ponse to a demand in America for well-made plates
of good design. Why we in England aren't considered
worthy of 'reprints' of the hundreds of English views
made at the same time, instead of some of the frightful
stuff you see in the CHINA shops nowadays – especially
the eternal standard variety of the WILLOW PATTERN –
I just don't understand.

Amber
Worth mentioning because it is so often confused with
ambergris, a waxy material which comes from sperm
whales.

True amber is called a semi-precious 'stone', though
in point of fact it is not a stone at all but a fossilized
resin, found in long-buried forests of fir-trees. Most

of it comes from such an ancient forest which lies
under the waters of the Baltic. It isn't always amber-
coloured: sometimes you find it almost black, while
there are also varieties in brown and orange shades.

Plain strings of amber beads were highly popular
wear during the aesthetic craze of the 'nineties, and
amber pipes are seen often enough. Curio hunters like
to find pieces in which flies and other insects have been
entrapped for centuries.

Apostle Jugs

These relief-decorated jugs in fine stoneware, together
with stablemates like the well-known MINSTER JUGS,
are – according to the way you look at them – either
Victorian vulgarity or rather fun. They typify a
whole class of pottery which the mid-Victorians were
very proud of, and bought in huge quantities.

The Apostle jugs are straight out of the Gothic
Revival, and show a frieze of the apostles standing in

Meighware apostle jug

niches with pointed arches. The chief maker was Charles Meigh, of the Old Hall, Hanley, who also produced many other designs in this moulded ware in classical as well as Gothic styles. So too, did many other potters, including Samuel Alcock, some of whose efforts showed the relief figures in white against a coloured ground. Another whole class features the running plant decorations so beloved of the time, with or without colour.

Here is a field where comparatively little systematic collecting seems to have been done so far. But anyone interested should not have any particular difficulty in finding their way, for not only did these makers usually impress their names on the wares, but sometimes also (or instead of) gave them the useful registry marks, which enable them to be dated and traced to a maker (see page 251).

'Barge' Teapots

These huge brown teapots, often with a miniature replica of themselves on the lid, belong to a family of wares which chiefly hail from around Burton-on-Trent. There are gallon and half-gallon teapots, jugs, and also large mugs called 'clouts'. I have one of the latter labelled 'M. E. Neal, Honington, 1895', so if any reader can claim descent, they may have it in return for more information. People still living in the area recall some of the small, often one-man potteries like that of 'Bossy' Mason, a jovial soul by all accounts who lived at a village called Jacks-in-the-Hole, near Midway; his name is often to be found on the pots. They get the name 'barge' pots because they were popular with the canal boat people passing through. I don't know when production ceased, but the last person to sell them, apparently, was a Mrs Anne

'Barge' teapot

Bonas, of High Street, Masham, who died about 1931. The latest date I have seen on a pot is 1914. Around Burton, these are called 'Rockingham' wares, after the brown glaze, but as the 'clouts' do not seem to be known there I suspect that at least some of the pieces were made elsewhere, perhaps in Staffordshire. An interesting line of research for a Midlander?

Barometers

A long lifetime can be spent tapping the glasses of barometers without getting any useful result, probably because few people understand how or why the thing works – and anyway prefer to look upon it as a pleasant piece of wall furniture, like a DELFTWARE plate or a COPPER warming pan.

They *can* be made to work, of course, if you take them to one of the scientific instrument people – and also find out how to read them. But even so I would much prefer a mercury one to the usual aneroid type. My favourite is old Admiral Fitzroy's model, patented in the 'eighties, where you have the column of mercury in front of your eyes (no nonsense about pretending it's a clock) and a storm glass and thermometer thrown in, all in that rather delightful 'Victorian scientific' style.

But if we are talking about furniture, there are some very handsome pieces about, considered *as* furniture. The early 'stick' barometers, which are simply cases for a vertical column, have some fine workmanship, especially in inlay work, and consequently make their price. But the more modest wheel barometers of the last century show first-rate cabinet-making, and are well worth the money for this alone.

Basaltes

One of the less expensive of the early wares. The relative unpopularity of basaltes today is due, I feel, to the fact that people sometimes overlook what black can do when accompanied, say, by cornflower blue or a fiery orange.

You have here a black pottery whose blackness is not even relieved by a glaze, as it is in what has become known as JACKFIELD WARE. On the other hand, it carries some superb relief decoration, and if you like the neo-classical styles popularized by its inventor, Josiah Wedgwood, you will admire the shapes of the vases and other ornaments, boxes, table wares and other items, not forgetting the busts.

Wedgwood named his discovery after the famous black basaltic rocks of the Giant's Causeway, in Northern Ireland, but many other potters cashed in on 'Egyptian Black', as it was popularly called.

Sometimes they decorated it with encaustic ('baked on') colours, in the style of Greek pottery. But it seems to me that if you are going to have something

black, you might as well go the whole hog. Try a few
pieces on that white-painted shelf.

Battersea Enamels

You usually need only to produce your wallet to be
shown a genuine 'Battersea' box.

But don't misunderstand what has by now become
strictly a trade term, not necessarily intended to deceive. Very, very few of the SNUFF BOXES, PATCH
BOXES, WINE AND CORDIAL LABELS, etuis, NEEDLE AND
THREAD cases, tiny animals and other toys, it seems,
even those in the great collections, actually came from
the small factory which operated at York House,
Battersea, for three years from 1753 to 1756. Most of
them, when they are genuinely old at all, came from
Bilston or Wednesbury, in South Staffordshire.

In these attractive things, made for the ladies and
gallants of the eighteenth century, the box or other
article was of copper, and surfaced with a kind of
opaque glass which was then decorated by hand
painting or by printing in the same way as STAFFORD-
SHIRE PRINTED EARTHENWARE, or PORCELAIN, i.e. with
inked paper transfers taken from copper plates. Landscapes and other pictures of the day were used, and
one whole class of them is devoted to tender messages
between lovers or mementoes of a trip to Bath or some
other popular resort.

The serious collector of these items does not seek
them in the junk shops, and when he looks elsewhere
some study is needed. For when a dealer says 'Battersea', you have to make sure that he means at least
'Bilston', and is not showing you something that was
made in Birmingham or Czechoslovakia just a few
years ago, or one made of porcelain rather than enamel
– much copied nowadays.

Battersea box

But, of course, if you just want a pretty box, go ahead and buy it. I don't suppose they'll ever come any cheaper than they are now.

Bedroom Crockery

Now is the time – while they're still cheap – to sort over all those hitherto despised items which, like WASH HAND STANDS, were banished when modern plumbing appeared. If you have not already discovered it for yourself, you may be astonished to know what junk shops can provide in the way of admirably shaped and decorated ewers and basins, shaving mugs, footbaths, even slop pails. I saw one of the

Ewer and basin

Slop pail

Shaving mug

latter, with beautiful gilded CHINOISERIES, and loaded with flowers, hanging from a balcony in Chelsea lately. There is even another article in this family to be found *under* the junk-shop tables; and if you balk at bringing one of these into the lounge I would remind you that Queen Marie Antoinette's chamber pot, exquisitely mounted as a vase with a boy on top, is one of the cherished possessions of a house belonging to the National Trust.

Nobody need be surprised, of course, to find good-quality pottery in this department, for all the best

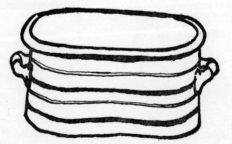

Footbath

Toilet table set

Victorian potters – Mintons and Wedgwoods among them – were in the trade, and gave of their best in it.

While still in the bedroom, it is worth taking another look at all those dressing-table sets, with trays, candlesticks, trinket and powder pots. A Worcester style popular early in the century, with flowers and gilding on faun-tinted china, is already in the shop windows.

Belleek

A porcelain from Fermanagh, in Ireland, covered with a glaze which some call pearly and glistening and others consider merely slimy. It is used for all kinds of wares, a favourite motif being the shell, which in fact its texture very much resembles. It is still being made today, marked with the name of the factory and a crest.

Bells, Bells, Bells

If you want to be posh you call them tintinnabula, so collecting them makes you a tintinnabulist.

This is one of those fields of collecting which don't make themselves apparent until you see an actual collection. But when you think that bells and gongs have been used in all ages all over the world for everything from fire engines to Buddhist shrines you can see what scope there is. (A gong, by the way, is something you hit with a hammer or other instrument: a bell has its own clapper – if it hasn't lost it.)

If you want to take your tintinnabulism seriously, of course, you need a yard, not a house. For, leaving aside the odd Indian temple bell brought back as a memento of service with the British Raj there are always ship's bells at Admiralty and merchant service break-up sales, old railway bells, school bells (there'll be more of these as they pull down village schools) and those fire bells that used to thrill us as the fire engine raced through the town. All these can make a grand noise, as can the brass or bronze gongs from the East, not all of them as mighty as the one at the beginning of the Rank films, but still capable of sending delicious throbbing reverberations round the district if you chose to call in some friends for a party.

Passing from the great crashers down to the tiny tinklers, the ones most frequently seen are the little BRASS call bells for the table, often with crinolined

Brass call bell

Peal of gongs

ladies whose legs are acting as clappers. There are
other figures as well including the Apostles, but here
many are being made again, and if you want to be
sure of having old ones you must inform yourself about
BRASS.

Also in this metal are the horse bells, in tiers, some
of them arranged as chords, used in association with
HORSE BRASSES. There are cow and wether bells,
dancers' bells, hand-ringing bells of the sort used to
give concerts in village pubs, kitchen bells ripped
out of old houses. There are also those call bells
which once stood on shop counters – you reached
up and banged the nob on the top when you wanted
someone to come and sell you a pennyworth of
sweets.

As to materials, the big ones, of course, are in bell
metal, an alloy of copper and tin. Then, apart from
brass, they come in such metals as antimony, SILVER,
gold. You can even find them in CHINA (GOSS included
them in his armorial range), in PORCELAIN (there is a
carillon of MEISSEN ones somewhere in Germany), and
of course, you will have seen many of the blue or red
'NAILSEA' ones.

Bianco Sopra Bianco

A very attractive decoration of DELFTWARE, in which a design is added in applied SLIP. The terms actually mean 'white over white', but more usually you find it with the decoration in white on a pale blue background.

Plates like this with bianco sopra bianco round the rim and a boldly painted flower in the centre are a dream. The TILES so decorated are a great feature of DELFTWARE from BRISTOL.

Bilston

The true South Staffordshire home of much that goes under the name of BATTERSEA ENAMELS.

Bird Call

A small pottery whistle in the shape of a bird. You blow through the tail, and in some cases, by wiggling the fingers, you can achieve the two-noted cuckoo call.

Sometimes the bird is found in a group, perching on a fence with her fledglings all around her. Sometimes she is built into a mug handle, a delight for children (and maybe the origin of 'wetting one's whistle').

Sometimes she is just a little bird of very ordinary clay, in which guise she has been found built into

Bird call

chimneys, to keep away hobgoblins and other things
that go boomp in the night.

Biscuit

A technical term used to indicate pottery and porcelain which has been left unglazed, or simply with a
smear glaze. It particularly applies to PORCELAIN
(both HARD PASTE and SOFT PASTE), which has also
been left 'in the white'.

It usually comes in the form of beautifully
modelled figures after eighteenth-century or classical
originals, and a Victorian attempt to recapture the
first fine careless rapture of early DERBY SOFT PASTE
BISCUIT figures led to the invention of PARIAN WARE.

Blanc-de-chine

Window-gazers are often stopped dead in their tracks
by figures of a Chinese lady in a most delightful sort
of white porcelain, beautifully modelled, and with a
serenity about her which you don't often find in the
Western World.

Blanc-de-chine (literally 'white of China') is
thought by many good judges to be the loveliest porcelain ever made. If it sounds unromantic to talk of
junket suddenly frozen in rhythmical curves, then
describe it for yourself. It isn't cheap, of course, and
it's getting dearer all the time.

As with CELADON, this is one of those items for when
that ship comes home, but just in case she does come
into harbour one of these days, let me tell you a little
more. It comes from Te-hua, in the province of
Fukien, and is sometimes known by either of those
names. Its whiteness has a wide range, right along
the colour circle from warm pink through the creams
to milky white, a smokey grey and a cold bluish tinge.

Kuan-yin in Blanc-de-chine

With that, and the polished glaze, it is no wonder that most of it was left 'in the white'; it would have been pointless to decorate it.

The lady mentioned above is Kuan-yin, by far the most popular of the figures. She seems to have been a very good sort, for she protected sailors from shipwreck, gave children to the childless, and interceded for those in hell. Even on her way into a much-deserved heaven she paused upon the threshold on hearing a cry of distress from some unfortunate. You often see her carrying in her hand a wand of *ju-i*, an instrument which will grant all your wishes for you – providing you deserve it, of course.

As I say, Blanc-de-chine is dear: one with the tiny delicate fingers of the hand repaired was offered me recently for sixteen pounds, while a small libation cup was five pounds. But I notice that in some shops there are figures of Kuan-yin in pottery, which are pleasant enough to look at.

'Blue and White'

This is a term you will often hear when pottery and

porcelain are being discussed. It could, however, refer to several different sorts, as follows:

1. CHINESE PORCELAIN sent to Europe in vast quantities from the seventeenth century onwards, decorated in cobalt blue under the GLAZE, and popularly known here as old NANKIN;

2. English PORCELAIN (SOFT PASTE) from factories like BOW, WORCESTER, LOWESTOFT, CAUGHLEY, etc. decorated by painting or transfer printing in blue under or over the GLAZE;

3. STAFFORDSHIRE PRINTED EARTHENWARE, bearing designs like the famous WILLOW PATTERN, landscapes, sporting scenes and the rest; or

4. DELFTWARE, either following the Chinese patterns with which it competed or with charming shipping and other scenes.

Why particularly '*blue* and white'? Before the nineteenth century cobalt was one of the few pigments which would stand up to the high temperatures of the potter's kiln: and after that, one supposes, because everybody copied everybody else. But also, no doubt, because it harmonizes so beautifully with wood, especially oak. Since oak went out of fashion, blue and white hasn't been so much appreciated here: but the Scandinavians, who still furnish a great deal with plain woods, have been buying all the above kinds for years. So be warned that if ever oak should become popular here again, you may find that all the 'blue and white' has disappeared into the blue.

Blue-Dash Chargers

A charger was a large plate or dish, on which one bore to the festive board the boar's head or other delicacy.

John the Baptist's head, you will recall, was brought before Herod on one, and if you still think, as I once did, that this particular charger was a horse I'm sorry to shatter an illusion.

The 'blue dash' part of it refers to the fact that many of these large DELFTWARE plates or dishes have a border of slanting blue dashes. The crude figures of kings and queens have never attracted me but I love the magnificently vital floral patterns in colours as fresh and lively as the day they were put on.

You'll be lucky to find any of these in a junk shop, but I mention them in case, by one of those miracles which is always occurring, you should find one in a pile of old earthenware.

Bone China
When you hear this expression used, someone is being technical about CHINA, which see.

Bottle Gardens
People are beginning to notice how very handsome are some of the big STONEWARE jars and glass carboys. And as many of these are being superseded by plastic containers, these big pots have begun to appear in the junk shops.

There's no need to wait for that, of course. A visit to Doultons' or one of the other manufacturers of chemical STONEWARE might open your eyes very much to the fine shapes and textures of these things, and how their very size and coarseness flatters the delicacy of your flowers and plants. I've no doubt at all that one day these things will be as seriously collected as salt-glazed STONEWARE or SLIPWARE is today.

As for the glass carboys, these are being used as miniature gardens. You may know that there is such a thing as a Wardian case – a glass affair, used for transporting plant specimens alive from one place to another. The carboy garden is a development of this idea; you put in some finely sifted soil, also some seeds of ferns and other plants, and providing you water them regularly and let them see the sun they will flourish like the green bay tree.

Bow

Probably the earliest of the English PORCELAIN (SOFT PASTE) factories, but definitely not for the likes of us, except by accidents and miracles – which nevertheless happen. The best place to see a lot of it is the Schreiber collection in the Victoria and Albert Museum, London.

Brass

There are two things to be said in favour of collecting brass. One is that your best bargains will generally be found in such a shocking state that after you've got them home and put in a little elbow grease on them, they seem to be worth at least twice as much as you've paid for them.

Brass candlesticks – early and late

The other is that if you boggle at the idea of regular cleaning, you can nowadays buy lacquer which keeps them bright. Having said which, let me tell you that I know at least two collectors who would rather die than lay a glistening coating over the subtle glow of old brass. Though never known to help with the smallest household chore (brass collectors are generally men) they will sit for hours indoors in the brightest weather, neglecting their lawns, their meals and (if they dared) their jobs while they fondle and polish their treasures.

But what to collect? I think you have first to make up your mind if you are interested in 'genuine' brass – or rather what you mean by that term. Brass, which in its modern sense is an alloy of two parts copper to one part zinc, seems not to have been made in England until late Elizabethan days, and it is worth noting that when Shakespeare said:

When sometimes lofty towers I see down-raz'd,
And brass eternal slave to mortal rage

he was talking about bronze, which didn't pick up its own name until about the middle of the eighteenth century. So here we have a curious example of an old product giving up its name to a new one, and taking another name for itself. Some etymologist collector may one day tell us where both these names come from, for the Oxford English Dictionary doesn't seem to know.

Anyway, if you want old brass, you must learn to distinguish between the earlier alloys and the way they are worked, i.e. if whether the piece was cast or hammered out of latten, the name given when the metal came in the form of sheets.

Not, perhaps, surprisingly, dealers seem to know a

Brass letter rack

lot less about metals than they do about CHINA or GLASS, though of course they are well aware of its scrap value, which is used as the basic yardstick of price. After that they look at workmanship, apparent age, curiosity or what not.

But if you study the subject at all, you will be well ahead of most of them except the specialist dealers, of which there are several among the members of the British Antique Dealers Association (see *Introduction*). With these, of course, you will be the humble learner, and must treat them respectfully, as if they were your family solicitors.

Again, what to collect? Well, there are all those miniature ornaments, such as tiny brass stools and fenders, etc., which Birmingham is still making industriously. There are BUTTONS, which are mentioned under that head; there are small brass DOOR KNOCKERS, which are also being made again. I like shape in all things, and there is a graceful water jug which is worth its position in any home, old or not; there are also helmet-shaped coal scuttles, andirons and other FIREPLACE FURNITURE.

Lifting your eyes from the fireplace to the cottage mantelpiece, there are those quite fascinating brass and other metal ornaments stamped out in the shape of figures, like horses, peacocks, shepherds. Sometimes

Brass tobacco tamper

you will find groups, like 'the goose that laid the golden egg'. (See PLAQUES.)

While on figures, don't overlook those amusing DOOR PORTERS of brass, or the little tobacco tampers which go right back to the beginning of pipe smoking in this country. Their business end is flat and small enough to press down the burning tobacco, but the other end can be in the shape of almost anything, from a king's head to a lady's leg.

Then there is the whole range of Oriental and African brass which will take you into realms of legend, ritual and religion and can keep you interested for several lifetimes. Here it is not so much a question of antiquity as of their intrinsic interest, for many of these pieces are being made still for their original purpose.

I must confess that I'd never really looked very closely at such things until one day when I chanced to be in a little bric-à-brac shop gazing round at a depressing assortment of Victorian china. Suddenly I saw a small brass group consisting of a very much elongated negro shooting a spear from a bow, with a dog attached to his leg. The pair seemed only that moment to have stepped out of a bush and were about to knock down a buck. As I didn't buy brass at that time, I went out without buying, but that hunter and his dog haunted me for days. Eventually I phoned the dealer in a panic (I had to ring the police to find out his name) and sent him the thirty shillings he wanted.

When the group arrived, of course, I desperately wanted to know all about it (see what I mean about collecting?). By poking about in places like the British Museum and that wonderful Pitt Rivers Museum at Oxford, I found that the group came from Dahomey, in West Africa, and had been made by a process known as *cire perdue*, or 'lost wax'. With this, a model is made in wax, which is then coated with fire-resisting clay. When fired the wax melts and runs out, leaving a hollow mould into which molten brass or bronze is poured. Thus, as will be seen, every piece is unique and unrepeatable. But there are many different subjects – chiefs walking in procession, mothers calling their children, men rowing in canoes. As I say, they're still being made, but I don't find that this worries me for here we're not collecting antiques, or things made in imitation of them, but little works of art illustrating the customs and habits and feelings of human beings – than which, of course, there is nothing more exciting.

In a similar field are those fascinating little gold weights from Ashanti: they're tiny brass figures in all sorts of grotesque and comic forms used as scales in the gold dust trade. These you will see more often in museums than the Dahomey figures, and I've yet to find my first one in a junk shop. But I'm looking!

Bristol
You will come across the name of the great West Country seaport in a number of fields, for it has been

a manufacturing centre since the Middle Ages. Here
are some of the things made there:

1. DELFTWARE, from 1650 down to about 1770,
especially in the suburb of Brislington. Styles are
similar to those of Lambeth and LIVERPOOL.

2. A rare and early PORCELAIN (SOFT PASTE), called
Lowdin's Bristol, and origin of the wares made at
WORCESTER.

3. PORCELAIN (HARD PASTE), made first at Plymouth
by William Cookworthy, who had invented it all over
again a thousand years after the Chinese and fifty
years after the Germans; then taken over at Bristol by
Richard Champion, who sold his patent to NEW HALL.

4. STONEWARE and EARTHENWARE of STAFFORD-
SHIRE types, notable among which was the creamware
decorated in bold bright enamels by William Fifield,
Jr., and often met with nowadays in the south-west.

5. A beautiful GLASS (OPAQUE), nothing like 'opaline' or even what is usually called milk glass, but
very similar in appearance to, and often mistaken for,
PORCELAIN. Now very much collectors' items and dear.

6. GLASS ('BRISTOL' BLUE) and other colours, made
also at Stourbridge and other centres.

Bronzes (and things like them)

Figures, groups and other objects cast in bronze are
unjustly neglected nowadays – unless they happen to
be collectors' items from, say, the Italian Renaissance
or Ancient China. A dealer friend tells me that this is
due to the fact that 'they ain't got no colour, which is
what the women wants, and what's the good of trying
to please men in this business?'

All the same, a pair of bronzes like the famous
Marly horses, from the marble originals by Guillaume
Cousteau (1677–1746), now in the Champs Elysées,

can look very dashing on your mantelpiece. If you can't afford the bronze version (which the dealer usually sells purely on its value *as* bronze) treat yourself to a pair in white metal for a couple of pounds. I have seen these painted white and turned into most effective lamp standards: I have also seen them gilded and placed upon the gate-posts of a house on a new building estate. This must have staggered the neighbours until they got used to it!

All this family of metal figures, never very expensive unless the metal is, wants turning over and examining with 'new' eyes. Although there is much sloppy sentiment, or 'phoney' posing, there are also charming little groups, especially of children and animals, well worth saving from the scrap heap and painting, either in white or in colours.

Buhl

I suppose we should really spell this word 'Boulle', for the special sort of metal MARQUETRY which goes under this name was introduced by a Frenchman named Andre-Charles Boulle (1642–1732).

This form of decoration, in which brass or copper (or sometimes pewter) is set alongside tortoise-shell, IVORY, bone or mother-of-pearl, continued to be popular right through the Victorian era. Some pieces were reproductions of the earlier work, some worked out Victorian ideas. Buhl clocks were especially popular, of course, and the prices asked for these nowadays are by no means excessive.

Buttons

I never thought buttons could be of any particular interest until one day in the Caledonian Market I came across a whole lot of them marked with different

Silver button

crests. I was told they were livery buttons, made for the household servants of the great ones of other days. Some of them were very handsome affairs, either in silver or gilt and there are many collectors whose delight and interest it is to get sets together and identify the person or family owning the crest – which, of course, can be done by turning up heraldry reference books.

Since then I've realized that there are many other kinds of buttons to be collected. Apart from naval and military ones, there are those worn by engine drivers, guards and other personnel of all the old railway companies, fire-brigades, shipping lines, etc. – the list is endless.

In craftmanship it is difficult to find anything better than the sporting buttons – hunt buttons struck with the name of the hunt and a fox mask; shooting and cock-fighting clubs had theirs as well.

So far as materials are concerned, there are the early silk and stuff ones, purely for ornament, while afterwards they come in BRASS, tin, PEWTER, COPPER, gold, SILVER, IVORY, GLASS, horn, tortoiseshell, bone. China ones were a speciality of MINTONS, while Wedgwoods made them in JASPER WARE.

Cadogan Teapot

This peculiar peach-shaped teapot, which comes in all sizes from miniature to giant, and is usually

Cadogan teapot

covered with a brown glaze, has no lid, and therefore
must be filled from the bottom, through a tube which
goes up inside the pot itself. It is said to be named
after a Lady Cadogan of the eighteenth century who
liked to make her guests guess how the tea got into the
pot. I have never tried to make a cup of tea in one,
but I should have thought that getting the tea-leaves
out presented a problem. The Chinese original from
which it was copied was probably a wine pot rather
than a teapot.

Cameo Shells

Here is an item which has shot up in value during
the past few years – the large conch or helmet shell
carved with cameo relief, sometimes rather like those
on JASPER WARE. A few years ago I picked one up for
about 10s., but now I see good specimens cost several
pounds.

They were highly popular as ornaments in Victorian
times and were made by the thousand, often by people
working in their own homes to the shell merchant's
orders. The decoration relies on the fact that the shell
is made up in layers of different colours, so that if you

c

Cameo shell

carve something in one layer, it stands out in relief against the next. Most of the designs were based on classical subjects.

The shells themselves came from the Indian Ocean and as well as being used in this way, the best parts were cut up to make Cameos and other SHELLWORK.

One of the most effective ways of dealing with these whole shells is to have the spiral inside cut out and mounted with a lamp, which lights up the design most effectively.

It may not matter to you very much but it is as well to realize that these items are still being made in Italy.

Can

In porcelain and pottery a cup becomes a *can* when it has no foot-rim; that is to say, has a flat bottom. Its sides may be either straight or shaped. The term is used mostly in talking of coffee cans, or drinking cans, to distinguish them from cups and mugs.

Plenty of cans, of all types and materials, with every kind of decoration, are to be had for shillings from the cupboards of antique shops.

Candle-stands

You will sometimes find lurking in the back of old furniture showrooms one, or possibly a pair, of these stands, upon tripod feet.

They may have spent most of their lives topped with a plant bowl in Victorian halls, but as likely as not they will have started life as candle-stands – or *torchères*, to give them their French name. They were used to give light in dark corners, or beside a boudoir table.

There are, of course, highly elaborate ones, carved, and sometimes gilded: these, and even the pretty little walnut ones with octagonal tops are now in the expensive furnishing shops. But the later and larger ones in mahogany are still about for ten pounds or so a

Candle-stand

pair, and they have possibilities, say, for the end of a corridor, or in a featureless corner of a large room. You could put plants on them, as no doubt their last owners did.

But why not give them one of those nice frosted glass Regency LAMPS? Burning oil, not the eternal converted electricity – it gives a much nicer light, especially for a party.

Canton

I have heard this term used in two ways, for ENAMELS from the decorating shops of Canton, notably the sort known as Cloisonné; and also for a type of CHINESE PORCELAIN. This latter is a very much (to some tastes) over-decorated nineteenth-century ware, which was painted in enamels and made especially for 'foreign devils' like you or me, but which no self-respecting Chinese would ever have in his house.

In the United States, I understand, this term is applied to what we would call NANKIN. What *they* call our CANTON I have no idea.

Card Cases

People who called on neighbours and acquaintances to 'leave cards' once carried these cards in beautiful little cases, made of almost every sort of decorative material. They came in tortoiseshell, inlaid pearl, ivory, PAPIER MÂCHÉ, mother-of-pearl, wood, metal, filigree, beadwork, Berlin work, moulded sealing wax and even SILVER and PORCELAIN.

One sees a good many of these little cases about, and not at all dearly priced, considering the workmanship which has been put into them – which I suppose we shall never see again lavished on such ordinary work-aday little affairs.

Card cases in papier mâché and mother-of-pearl

One reason they're so cheap (a pound or two will buy a nice one) is that they're usually just too small to take cigarettes, and there aren't many other practical uses one can make of them. But they can look most attractive when set out on a black velvet tray; so if you like beautiful workmanship, why not gather some together – before we all start leaving cards on each other again and they disappear from the shops?

Carpet Balls

You will occasionally come across a set, or more likely a few specimens, of a sort of china ball with coloured rings. These were used on long TV-less Victorian evenings for the game of Carpet Bowls. For this you needed one plain and six patterned balls, or 'taws', which were in fact usually made of STONEWARE or EARTHENWARE.

You also need a fairly long corridor to play the game in style, so if you become the owner of a set you really ought to buy a baronial mansion as well.

Castleford

Here is another of those wares which are so

Castleford teapot

characteristic in shape and looks that you can spot specimens from the top of a bus.

To my mind, Castleford is quite unjustly neglected, both by collectors and historians, and I for one would like to know a great deal more about it.

Not all these fine STONEWARE teapots and other wares, decorated with panels in relief and sparingly lined in colours, were made at Castleford, though David Dunderdale & Co., of that Yorkshire town, seem to be the principal makers and impressed their name or initials in the ware.

It is held that pieces with convex (bulging) corner panels are indubitably Dunderdale or at least Castleford-made, whereas those with concave panels and a number impressed were made elsewhere. But, as I say, information is scanty, and there is room for informed collecting. Pieces are not cheap, but considering their attractiveness, their charming period flavour and their rank in the STONEWARE hierarchy, prices are certainly not excessive at, say, five pounds for a teapot.

Castles
Are put in their place (so far as pottery ones are concerned) behind COTTAGES.

Caughley

People talk about Caughley (or 'Salopian') as one of the lesser lights of early English PORCELAIN (SOFT PASTE). 'Even Caughley', they say, in a derogatory sort of way. For me, if I were going to collect SOFT PASTE seriously I think I should go in for Caughley just because of this.

But it's a ware which brings its own rewards as well. The factory (at least the porcelain part of it) was started by that Thomas Turner of WILLOW PATTERN fame and whose story is told under that head. He learned his business of potting at WORCESTER, so not surprisingly the early wares are similar to those of the Severn town.

The WORCESTER hollow 'C' mark was imitated, also the WORCESTER imitations of CHINESE; but 'S' or 'Salopian' was the factory's own mark and in 1799 it was purchased by John Rose of COALPORT.

Celadon

Here is a ware to buy if you are expecting to be poisoned. It is a type of CHINESE PORCELAIN (or the colour of its GLAZE) which is reputed to change colour if poisoned food or drink is put in it.

It changes colour quite enough as it is, for although in theory it is a greyish olive green, you find it in most shades of green from grey to blue. Some say it was named from a character in a French comedy of the eighteenth century, a shepherd who wore a costume of this colour: some say that it derived from Saladin, on the ground that that Islamic monarch ordered a great deal of it from China.

You are unlikely to find much of it going cheaply but it's heavenly stuff and everybody ought to have a piece of it. So whenever you have a ship come home

treat yourself to one of those large bowls with little
fishes in relief swimming round the sides.

Chelsea

Home of probably the most delightful of English
PORCELAIN (SOFT PASTE), but if you find any Chelsea
in a junk shop either the dealer is fast asleep or you
are dreaming beautiful dreams.

For what it's worth, however, you may like to
memorize the mark at the back of the book, remem-
bering that not only have potters reproduced Chelsea
in BONE CHINA, but that it was even copied by distinguished people like COALPORT – which would make
the ware collectable in its own right.

Children's Plates

Not to be confused with toy china, which were miniatures of adult sets, or with travellers' samples, which
were tiny versions or half-pieces, of the real thing,
carried by peripatetic salesmen. These are plates made
directly for use by children, and embellished with decorations designed to amuse, elevate or interest them.

As might be expected, not many have survived. The
potters don't seem to have expected them to, for they
are generally found in the cheapest sort of earthenware. If they were ever made in STONEWARE (as
you'd imagine they would be, in view of the hazardous
life they were in for), I haven't seen them.

Surprisingly enough, however, they *can* still be
found, and although you sometimes see them in
antique shops marked up at several pounds, the real
place to seek them is the darkest corner of the dingiest
junk shop, under piles of old saucers (which, by the
way, you should never, never, leave un-turned over).

Some of these charming items are designed for the

Davenport child's plate

very young, with impressed numbers or letters of the alphabet round the rim. Others are seemingly for more advanced infants, as they offer counsel on matters of behaviour up to the age of marriage – though often still keeping up the alphabetical instruction. Pictures and verses recommended virtues like modesty, propriety and industry, but some potters like DAVENPORT were charitable enough to let the child uncover pictures of animals as he spooned up his food.

A series which has been paid the compliment of a place in the Victoria and Albert Museum, London, is called 'Flowers that Never Fade', and really gets down to the 'seen and not heard' business. Two typical verses run:

ATTENTION

And when I learn my hymns to say
And work and read and spell
I will not think about my play
But try to do it well.

POLITENESS

If little boys and girls were wise
They'd always be polite
For sweet behaviour in a child
Is a delightful sight.

Apart from DAVENPORT, many potters seem to have made these items, notably the Newbottle Pottery in Sunderland. But there is still much to be learned about them, and they could make an engrossing field for collecting.

Has anyone ever thought of poking about in the gardens of old cottage sites in the country? There must be many fragments there which could be pieced together.

China

I have heard this overworked word used to describe almost everything in ceramics except a flower pot. So shall we have a quick canter round the crockery and sort out some terms?

Although a 'potter' makes all kinds of ceramics, the word 'pottery' is usually used to describe ceramic products which cannot be classed as PORCELAIN. The basic material is clay of one kind or another.

When you bake clay in a kiln, it becomes EARTHEN-WARE, like your flower pots. If you bake it even harder, i.e. at much higher temperatures, the clay vitrifies (shall we say 'glassifies'?) and you have STONEWARE, as in a hot water bottle.

PORCELAIN is a sort of refined stoneware made from two forms of felspathic rock fused together, HARD PASTE being the 'true' variety invented originally by the Chinese and SOFT PASTE the substitute used in eighteenth-century Europe until the Chinese version

was rediscovered. In England, however, except at
Plymouth, NEW HALL (doubtfully) and BRISTOL we
never got around to using HARD PASTE at all, but instead evolved our own unique BONE CHINA which is, in
fact, the standard English CHINA. This was developed
by Josiah SPODE II, among others, and contains
bone ash, not in the small proportions used by some
of the SOFT PASTE factories, but anything up to 40 per
cent of the whole 'mix'. To know what it looks like,
buy an ordinary cup and saucer at a china shop.

Other bodies known under the name of CHINA are
STONE CHINA and even sometimes PARIAN, information
about which can be gleaned by following the
CAPITALS.

A note on CHINA PATTERNS

Many and wonderful are the patterns which potters
have evolved to make us desire their wares, and it
would need several books to discuss half of them. You
can hunt a great many down by means of the works
in the READING LIST, but there is still a great deal of
guesswork to be done, especially in the Victorian era.

When trying to identify pottery or porcelain by
their patterns remember that copyright is a fairly
modern invention. In other days potters have always
been cheerfully unscrupulous about stealing each
other's patterns, sometimes giving them a fresh twist,
sometimes not bothering even to do that.

Furthermore, if English potters have followed Continental and Chinese themes (*cf.* the famous WILLOW
PATTERN), so these others have, when it suited them,
copied ours. The Chinese have even carried this a
stage further by imitating our imitations of *their* work.
So it never does to be too quick to jump to con-
clusions, however typical a piece may look.

This glorious tangle, of course, gives lifelong employment to the expert dealer, endless delight to the connoisseur, and bafflement to the tyro. The only real way to cope with the situation is to plunge right in, buy, and hope for the best. It's surprising how soon a few purchases will teach you how wrong you can be, and how quickly, if you persevere on this course, you will learn to recognize the maker of a STAFFORDSHIRE PRINTED EARTHENWARE plate by the flowers round the border, or a DERBY plate by the way a painter handles the tones on a rose petal.

China Figures

A shop full of china figures (or figurines, as they're sometimes called) can be a baffling thing to a beginner. Where on earth do you start? How can you possibly find your way through all that undergrowth of DRESDEN shepherdesses, monkey bandsmen, highwaymen, Jenny Linds and the rest?

I think you start by looking hard at them, and then, very cautiously, buying things you like. You may not like them later on, but as most things are appreciating in value, this may not necessarily involve a loss when you sell.

Then you should read up something about them from the experts, and even compare them with other kinds of figures – say sculpture or BRONZES.

You will find, of course, that it occurred to man very early on to want to make likenesses of other people, also of animals and gods. At first there was some motive like giving a dead person an attendant on his journey into the next world. Later, the potter found that people liked to have these things while they were still in this world – to put on their mantelpiece or decorate their tables.

What the earliest potters made are either in the big collections or still under the ground waiting to be uncovered by the archaeologist. In the cabinets of the well-off, too, are those delicious BLANC-DE-CHINE figurines of the Chinese immortals, the breath-takingly fragile and graceful figures from the Italian Comedy modelled at MEISSEN by Kaendler or at Nymphenburg by Bustelli (which can cost you £4,000 a whack at Sotheby's!); the charmingly anglicized versions of Continental ideas made in our own PORCELAIN (SOFT PASTE) factories like BOW, CHELSEA, DERBY, Longton Hall etc.; the delightfully naïve early salt-glazed STONEWARE figures as shown in the famous pew-groups and bandsmen; the earthenware products of potters like Astbury and Whieldon, dripping with glorious coloured glazes apparently thrown on from the other end of the room but all the same arriving at exactly the right spot: there, too, even, are the comparatively late figures of Obadiah Sherratt and Ralph Salt.

So what we are left with nowadays mainly are, *first*, nineteenth-century imitations of the eighteenth-century porcelain figures; *second*, the STAFFORDSHIRE CHIMNEY ORNAMENTS of the nineteenth century (which are discussed under that head); *third*, a sprinkling of original figures made by DOULTONS, Pilkingtons and others in the last eighty years or so; *fourth*, PARIAN figures, still making only a few pounds; and *fifth*, a whole selection of items made the other day from the original moulds, still coming out of Europe and Staffordshire wrapped up in their original tissue paper.

'Chinese'
When a European paints a flower on a vase, or a little

Chinese-style Spode plate

fish upon a bowl, it is, like Wordsworth's primrose, a flower or a fish and nothing more.

But when a Chinese potter does it, there is a meaning to it: he is spelling out a message, as a sailor does with flags. A conch shell, for example, means a prosperous journey; a pair of fishes indicates domestic felicity. A magnolia tree, a quince and a peony can be put together to read: 'May you dwell in jade halls and enjoy wealth and honours.'

Much of this sign language is built up on a system of punning, which the Chinese love no less than the English: for example, the spoken word for peach sounds the same as that for long life, while the word citron sounds like 'happiness'.

So when you come across a collector of 'Chinese', wrapped up in his Eight Immortals, his Lions of Fo, Kylins and other animals, gods or humans, you will understand why he feels slightly sorry for those of us who plod around in the humdrum foothills of European wares.

The Chinese, of course, were the first PORCELAIN makers – by nearly a thousand years. And all the way down to the present day the best of their work – usually that made for themselves, not that made for exportation to the 'foreign devils' – has been supreme for strength, beauty, delicacy and an immensely 'professional' look and feel.

If you want to be able to recognize it at once, go to a dealer and get him to show you three plates, all with 'BLUE AND WHITE' Chinese designs on them, and in fact all made within a century of each other – but otherwise vastly different. One could be a typical Chinese export plate, as described under NANKIN – hard, brilliant, probably with an unglazed foot-rim, perhaps a little pitted, and with glaze and body fused into one material. The next would be in soft earthen-

Chinese plate

Yi-Hsing stoneware teapot

ware, showing grey or brown where the opaque tin-enamel has flaked off, painted in a dashing rather than a meticulous style – this is DELFTWARE, made in England or Northern Europe in imitation of the Chinese ware. The third plate would also be EARTHENWARE, but of the STAFFORDSHIRE PRINTED variety, much lighter than the Chinese one, but with a more crowded Chinese-style design – as likely as not the WILLOW PATTERN, surrounded by an uncompromisingly English border of roses. When you've compared these three plates for material, style and feel, you'll never confuse them again.

But apart from the BLUE AND WHITE wares there are other kinds of Chinese porcelain, according to the length of your purse. The lovely white BLANC-DE-CHINE has already been mentioned, but look out also for the pots with 'self-coloured' or monochrome glazes with names like 'peach-bloom', 'mirror-black' and 'tea-dust'. You could refer also to CRACKED ICE, CRACKLE GLAZE, LOWESTOFT, NANKIN, PORCELAIN. And if you should come across a little red stoneware teapot

shaped like the one in the drawing, you may like to
know that it is descended from the earliest ones ever
to come into this country, with the first consignments
of tea in the seventeenth century. And good judges
claim that it makes the best cup of tea of any!

Chinese marks are a special study. Some indicate
the reign in which the piece was made, but these were
often imitated on later wares. Others signify the purpose for which the piece was made. The main periods
are T'ang (618–906 A.D.), Sung (960–1279) Yüan
(1280–1368), Ming (1368–1644) and Ch'ing (1644–
1912).

Your happy hunting ground, unless you are pretty
well off, will be in the Ch'ing, and pretty late on in
that too: but that is not to say you mightn't come
across something from the earlier dynasties. One thing
to remember is that most general dealers keep back
their Chinese pieces against the visit of a specialist or
his runner. But if you make a friend of him yourself
and pay him his price, he may keep them for *you*.

'Chinoiseries'
Nobody can browse in antique shops for long without
becoming aware that somewhere about the year 1740
Europe was hit by something which has been described as 'China-mania'. It took the form of decorating PORCELAIN, printing chintzes and embroidering
pictures with fantastic Chinese-style landscapes and
figures (see LONG ELIZAS). It brought us lacquer furniture and Chinese CHIPPENDALE; it started off the
WILLOW PATTERN on its long career; it built the Brighton Pavilion and the pagoda in Kew Gardens (Surrey),
both of which stand today as living memorials to
it.

Other countries were purged of this aberration by

Chinese Chippendale

the revival of classical styles at the end of the eighteenth century. But despite the strenuous efforts of tycoons like Josiah Wedgwood – who found that neoclassical severities suited mass production methods better than more fanciful things – English people never really did recover from it – look, for example, at the WILLOW PATTERN! Even when they did, it was only to get bowled over again by it in the 'EMPIRE' period, and then by still another wave of orientalism – the 'Japanesy' vogue of the eighteen-seventies and eighties – which you will find in pilgrim bottles from WORCESTER, MINTONS, AND DOULTONS, in furniture of slender form, in lacquer, stamped leather and bamboo.

None of these outbreaks was based on the true art of either China or Japan, the natives of which country took care never to have in their own homes the things they sent us. What it represented really was the English dream of all ages – the longing for a fantastic nevernever land as far away as possible, where there are no fogs, no taxes, no overcrowded buses. In fact, nothing to do all day but sit upon a crazy, crumbling bamboo structure under a wide sun-shade and be fanned by a ravishing little creature with a lotus blossom in her hair.

Chippendale

You'll have a job to buy a real Chippendale chair in a junk shop, but if you say 'chippendale', you'll be shown something with flowing curves, plenty of carving and in most ways as different as possible from HEPPLEWHITE and SHERATON. Thomas Chippendale (1718–1779) was a highly successful cabinet maker who ran a flourishing and fashionable business in St Martin's Lane, London, and who published a collection of designs in *The Gentleman and Cabinet Maker's Director*. Although many ideas once attributed to him are now known to be the work of others, his name remains for the style.

Chippendale chair

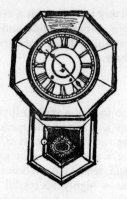

18th century wall clock

Clocks

There are men who cannot resist picking up a stopped clock and feeling they want to do something about it.

So I don't think there's much point in saying a great deal about the sort of clocks you see in junk or small general antique shops. If you're interested in clocks at all you'll either know a great deal more about them than I do, or you'll want to rush in anyway.

But I would like to air a few personal enthusiasms. First of all, perhaps, for grandfather clocks – and by the very fact of using that term at all you'll know I'm a tyro in this field like you: an expert would use the old name which was 'longcase' or 'tall' clocks. 'Grand-father', like Christmas and Mr Weller, seems to have come in with Dickens, or even later.

Anyway, there they are, the long and the fat and the tall – hopelessly unsuitable, I suppose, for modern surroundings, although I sometimes wonder if we've *quite* as little room as we pretend to have. For example

I'm at this moment (as it happens) sitting in a modern room with a ceiling high enough to take the tallest grandfather *I've* ever seen.

Of course, like you and everyone else, I'd like one of the early Jacobean ones, with the plain case and the tiny square dial: but these cost money, and so do the later walnut and MARQUETRY ones. But there are some fine specimens about in the larger and later sorts at anything from twelve pounds upwards – and if you feel that's a lot of money, think of your children. Wouldn't you love to have been brought up in a home where there was a great mysterious monster at the end of the hall ticking away the endless minutes of childhood? (Shame on you, go out and buy them one!)

Then there are some pretty good specimens of the plainer sorts of wall clock. You find some splendid movements in this rather austere type, probably intended for butlers' pantries or the offices of the Cheeryble brothers. If you don't happen to like the

Early 30-hr. wall clock

Georgian long-case clock

case there are always nice cases whose movement have long since gone to glory. And don't be too fussy about 30-hour movements (this applies to long-case clocks as well). For some reason people will always pay disproportionately more for an eight-day than a thirty-hour movement.

If you want to get really cottage, there are all those cheap glass-fronted clocks which were sent over here by the shipload from the United States in mid-Victorian times. Except possibly for pressed glass this must have been the earliest example of American mass-production methods, for one of the manufacturers, Chauncey Jerome, of Connecticut, got them over here so cheaply that the Customs accused him of undervaluing his wares – they cost only a few shillings each. So they bought up the shipment at his price – which so delighted Mr Jerome that he promptly sent another load, after which the Customs took his word for it. These clocks have a glass painting on the front as a rule, often with a faded instruction sheet inside at the back. They work on the weight system, strike chimes, and there's many a one in pub and parlour which has been ticking away steadily for a good century or more. I bought one of these for a pound, paid thirty shillings to have it put right, and it is pretty nearly the best timekeeper I have.

Talking about getting clocks put right, not everybody realizes that tucked away at the backs of towns, or even in villages, there are old clock repairers, mostly working for the antiques trade, who will perform miracles for really rather trifling sums. And since clocks, on the whole, are today under-valued rather than otherwise, I do invite you to have a closer look at all those Victorian mantelpiece clocks, some of them presentation items, which have survived their proud recipients. There are some good ones about, and if some of them are extravagant, it's surprising what a little careful redecoration can do.

Victorian mantelpiece clock

Coalbrookdale

A name found sometimes on COALPORT china, but
also the name of an ironfounding company which was
right in the forefront of the Victorian craze for ironwork, the bigger and more lavishly decorated the
better.

Coalport

A wonderful example of the way an unlovely name
can pick up, by association, a pleasing sound. 'Coalport' now signifies for most of us those fine tea and
dinner services with green and rose-coloured grounds
which were made all through last century, and in
fact, are still being put out by the company's successors in the factory's new (since 1926) home in
Staffordshire.

The earlier wares, of course, are the preserves of the
well-off collector. The factory was founded in 1796
by John Rose, a porcelain tycoon like Duesbury of
Derby, who started as an apprentice of Thomas
Turner of CAUGHLEY, and afterwards bought that
factory and also the Cambrian Pottery at SWANSEA –
and with it the heart-breakingly lovely porcelains

Coalport china pot-pourri

made by the famous and luckless Billingsley. With all this gathering of potting know-how COALPORT was in an excellent position to imitate CHELSEA, DRESDEN and other styles and to join in the extravagances of ROCKINGHAM in the way of applied flower decoration. Some people blench at some of this: some find it Fun. The Victoria and Albert Museum have canonized it by putting it in their cases, so who are we to talk scathingly about 'Revived Rococo?'

Cockle Plates

It may not be realized that museums often have a huge surplus of items of lesser importance tucked away in cupboards; and that they are usually quite glad to show them to anyone interested.

It was while exploring one of these hoards – acquired by the museum as a legacy on condition that they didn't just pick out the choice bits they wanted but took the lot – I saw piles and piles of engaging little plates of the shape and size one sees on cockle and whelk stalls. But instead of being plain, as they are today, they were printed with pleasant views, or with mottoes and cheerful pictures of sailors, rather like SOUVENIR CHINA. No doubt many of them did find their way into pockets on boisterous Saturday nights.

Some of them were rather larger than this, with rims impressed with rosettes in the same way as CHILDREN'S PLATES. Still others bore the emblems of Oddfellows and other societies, suggesting that they were used for ceremonial high teas. Rummaging around for little items of this sort – which, after I had seen this collection, I remembered having passed over many times – could take you along a fascinating by-path of social history.

Copeland

A famous name in pottery, but one which goes more
appropriately with another and perhaps more famous
one, which it has partnered now for over a century,
i.e. SPODE.

Copper

There are people who know old copper from new, but
not many who know *how* old and *how* new. I can take
you to shops which do a roaring trade in copper
'antiques' fresh from their factory tissue paper – all
those fascinating little miniature toys, hunting horns
for fox hunts and beagles, kettles, pots, scuttles and the
rest. They're all coming off a production line which
uses much the same sort of tools and processes as in
the old days.

And does mere age matter all that much? There's a
demand for copper: why not meet it? After all, if a
hunt wants to buy a new horn you don't expect them
to take the pack all round the Brighton Lanes in
search of a new one. (By the way, what happens to

Copper jug

the old ones? Do they get dropped down the foxholes?)
And if someone wants to buy some pretty miniature
kettles or warming pans at the seaside, isn't it nice to
think that you're buying some Birmingham workman
a Sunday dinner?

But if you *should* want something other than just
copper: if you want that authentic glowing red of the
old work, if you're attracted by a shape that just
couldn't have been made by a modern hand, then
that's a different matter. In this case I invite you to
look closely at all those oddly shaped and rather
crazily finished pieces; those oddities like muff war-
mers and beer mullers, sets of West Country measures,
PLAQUES, Victorian grille work, LAMPS and lanterns.
Look especially for signs of hand repairs by the old
coppersmiths and travelling tinkers; study their
methods of workmanship, good and bad.

Cottages and Castles
People who do not have to live in them have always
loved a cottage, from the days when Georgian ladies
and gentlemen built themselves tiny 'Gothick' ones in
their parks and played at being milkmaids and shepherds. In Victorian days, as working and middle-class
people herded themselves into towns, they too thought
wistfully of the charming little nests they had left behind them, set in gardens full of hollyhocks and sweet
william.

From these yearnings, pottery and china manufacturers reaped a rich harvest, and because these tiny
edifices were generally left in peace on a mantelshelf
or in a cabinet, a great many have come down to us.

Some are in the form of pastille burners, used to
sweeten the air of small, stuffy rooms. Others were
designed as night-light holders, a great convenience

when you had no electric light switch. But as time went on they were made frankly as ornaments, for MONEY BOXES, DOORSTOPS, TEA CADDIES, TEAPOTS, TOBACCO JARS, inkstands, watch holders – in fact, almost anything which occurred to the fertile minds in the hundreds of little potteries which made them all through the Victorian era.

Larger versions were made frankly as ornaments, for the sideboard or the mantelpiece, and coming in such variety and being relatively cheap, they made excellent presents. Apart from the cottages there were castles, churches, tollhouses, garden arbours, summerhouses etc. Some of the best of them, considered as pieces of intricate and elaborate potting, came from ROCKINGHAM, COALPORT, WORCESTER and DERBY between 1820 and 1840. These are making money now, whereas the more rudimentary ones are still to be bought for a couple of pounds.

But beware! the forger is here as elsewhere. In a junkshop in Staffordshire itself recently I was shown a cottage with all the signs of age on it, which the dealer – a secondhand furniture man really – told me laughingly had been made a few weeks before by a

Rockingham cottage

Staffordshire castle

pottery down the road, using the original Victorian moulds. It was a pretty good attempt, both in potting and decoration, but you could see a difference if you knew what to look for. So here, as elsewhere, the serious collector must go to the trouble of studying materials and styles. Start with the Reading List.

Cracked Ice

One of the most familiar of Chinese patterns, probably because it is still used on the famous BLUE AND WHITE ginger jars, which we have been buying at Christmas for many generations.

Not everybody knows that it symbolizes the Chinese New Year, which occurs in the spring when nature is re-awakening after its winter sleep. The broken slabs of deep blue represent the winter ice cracking on the lakes and rivers, while against this background is seen the prunus, or wild plum blossom – not, by the way, hawthorn, as is often thought.

The pattern is also seen on large vases, plates and other wares, and it has even been repeated on STAFFORDSHIRE PRINTED EARTHENWARE, though totally without the liveliness of the Chinese versions.

Crackle Glaze

A deliberate cracking of the glaze in CHINESE and some modern European PORCELAIN, for decorative effect.

Seen mostly in CELADON wares, it is a case of the potter taking advantage of a hazard in pot-making – in this case, the fact that if you don't look out, the glaze will cool at a different rate from the body and cause cracks to appear all over the surface. Sometimes a single piece will have two sets of 'crackle', one small and the other large.

Not to be confused with 'crazing', an imperfection in the ware, or the sign of long and honourable usage, as with Aunt Jemima's teapot.

Creamware, Cream-Coloured Earthenware

Here is another of the aristocrats of English pottery and almost the most delightful of them. Nobody who has ever once handled, say, one of the early teapots, with its deep buttery glaze, with crabstock handles and spouts, with painting in the vigorous, native Staffordshire tradition providing the most lovely harmonies and attractive discords, can ever mistake it for anything else.

It arose in Staffordshire, somewhere about 1720–40, made of the same materials as – but fired at a lower temperature than – the hitherto successful SALTGLAZED STONEWARE, which it slowly overhauled for all kinds of reasons which one hasn't room to mention here but which can be pursued in the Reading List.

The early pieces, of course, have long since gone into the museums or into the Sotheby class, and you have to be very lucky to find them by chance. But, with a little perseverance and especially if you don't mind a crack or a chip here or there, it is still possible to find some modestly priced pieces for a shelf. You certainly won't be sorry, for it grows on you day by day.

There is a wide range to choose from, even among the later wares, when Wedgwood was developing his famous 'Queen's Ware', with its clean neo-classical lines and restrained, but finely judged, decoration, and when LEEDS and other potteries were turning out the pieces in the pierced decoration for which they were noted.

Then there are those much more modest – most of them probably forever unidentifiable – plates, dishes and bowls, impressed with basket weave and other designs, picked out sparingly in blue, brown or green. They are still only valued at a pound or two, and they fill a shelf beautifully.

But don't *insist* on a Wedgwood mark, which many

Wedgwood creamware basket

Dish in cream-coloured Leeds ware

of them have. Dealers always ask more when they can show you a mark, and there was just as good cream-ware made outside Etruria as inside it.

Cup Plates

Once upon a time, when we used tea cups without handles, it was actually considered good form to drink from your saucer, which in fact was made deeper for the purpose, sometimes almost like a small basin.

All the same you weren't expected to plonk your cup down on the hostess's snowy linen. So she provided you with a little plate about three to four inches in diameter.

These cup plates, as they are called, come in either glass or earthenware, but they don't come so often as they did, for the Americans have been collecting them for a long time. Some carry the usual patterns of STAFFORDSHIRE PRINTED EARTHENWARE, and the marks of potters like Adams, Ridgway, Wood, Clews etc. The glass ones are sometimes quite plain, and sometimes in colour, with impressed patterns.

Cutlery

In most junk shops you will find a box full of knives, forks, spoons, skewers, perhaps liberally mixed up with bradawls, screwdrivers and a baby's dummy or two. These boxes are always worth looking into, for you may very easily come across something interesting in the cutlery line.

Of course, anything the dealers have been able to identify, like sterling silver, will have gone – or not been put there at all. But there are sometimes Victorian fish and fruit knives, beautifully engraved even if they are in electro plate, some of them with ivory or pearl handles. Bread knives are often quite splendid affairs, many being finely carved in boxwood.

A great deal of this work was done in living-rooms in the back streets of Sheffield by independent workers. Like the buffalo horn and stag handles, they date from before the days of the celluloid which one remembers smelling so frightfully when it got burnt on the stove.

Not so often come by, but worth building up into sets, are the earlier knives and forks with the shapes shown in our sketch, with steel blades and steel bone handles.

Spoons, of course, come in great variety. If you find a wooden one with fine carving on it you have the original spoon itself, for the word comes from the Old English 'spon', meaning a splinter of wood. But

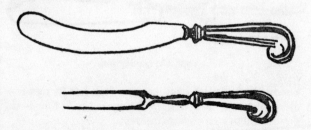

Georgian scimitar-bladed knife and two-pronged fork

Sealtop spoon

Victorian carving fork

almost every design of spoon and fork has its name –
there are over 200 designs being made today – so
there is plenty to engage interest.

Don't despise the occasional PEWTER one you may

find. Cleaned up and mounted – as they should be – on a spoon rack, which can be made by any handyman, they can look quite splendid. And if you should stumble across one of those with a Royal portrait on it, or with acorn, maidenhead or sealtop knops, you will soon have serious collectors breathing over your shoulder.

Davenport

A factory established by John Davenport at Longport, Staffordshire, in 1793, and continued under his descendants until 1882.

Several kinds of EARTHENWARE, STONE CHINA and BONE CHINA were made there, and decorations ranged from NEW HALL and other 'cottage' styles through IMARI to sumptuous affairs in the manner of DERBY. Some fine painted landscapes can still be found, though they will not be cheap now, while the charming CHILDREN'S PLATES with Zoo animals are also to be seen.

There are as well some delectable little LUSTRE WARE tea-sets. Marks usually include either the name of the firm, or the town, and an anchor.

Delftware

Sometimes you will see in a china shop, or perhaps in one of those places by the seaside where they sell SOUVENIR CHINA, a piece of glazed blue and white pottery, probably in the form of a little Dutch boy or girl, and marked 'Delft'.

The one thing you can be certain of is that this is not old DELFTWARE, for the potters who made this did not use the name. Old Delftware, English or Continental, is a coarse earthenware, often pitted, covered with an opaque tin glaze, and usually decorated in a quick,

Delftware apothecary jar

sure style of painting – made necessary by the painter's having to work on an absorbent surface. It gets its name from the Dutch town where a great deal of it came from, but actually it was made in England long before the rise of Delft, the principal centres here being Lambeth, BRISTOL and LIVERPOOL.

Those who like fine porcelain, laboriously painted, may find the free styles of Delft difficult to take, and in fact, it is generally considered a man's pleasure rather than a woman's. But it has its fanatical supporters, all busily pushing the price up – though it's still, I think, a good investment, for nothing like it could ever be made again. To do that we would have to re-create not only the materials of those days but the men who wielded those dashing brushes and mixed those wonderfully vivid colours.

Outstanding among the styles are the BLUE AND WHITE landscapes and seascapes, the CHINOISERIES with which the delftmakers tried to stem the tide of imported CHINESE PORCELAIN; the early polychrome plates, brightly and vigorously painted with tulips and other flowers; and the items mentioned under BLUE DASH CHARGERS: while apart from the plates (although one ought also to mention those with scalloped or gadrooned edges and with BIANCO SOPRA BIANCO decoration) there are those beautifully shaped early wine bottles, predecessors of SEALED BOTTLES in glass, also the puzzle jugs referred to under JOKE POTTERY, and the apothecaries' jars often seen in posh pharmacists' windows. Then there are TILES and PLAQUES, mentioned under those heads.

This ware is so old now that nobody minds a chip or two; and in fact I find them all a part of its charm: you certainly never notice them on a wall as you might with CHINA or PORCELAIN. But if you do hang old delft on the wall, don't use those gadgets which hook over the rim: they chip the glaze away rather *too* much.

And don't grudge it if you have to pay several pounds for a nice plate. A few years ago, 'Old Elson', as he liked to be called, of Christmas Steps, Bristol, offered me a pair of tulip plates for sixteen pounds, but not having then acquired a taste for delft I was foolish enough to think I couldn't afford it. Now, of course, so high has polychrome delft gone that I really can't afford it!

It may be well to point out in this place that what we in Northern Europe call Delftware is known in France as FAIENCE and in Italy as MAIOLICA, although the styles of these two wares are totally different from ours.

Derby
One of the earliest and most celebrated of English porcelain factories, founded by William Duesbury, an eighteenth-century "take-over" specialist, who bought up CHELSEA, BOW and some smaller unrecorded places. Figures were made in the styles already set by CHELSEA and a lovely porcelain was evolved for table wares.

CHELSEA-DERBY is the name used for wares made from about 1770, when the London firm, together with its moulds and workmen, were acquired. There was some wonderful flower-painting, and notable among the productions of this time was the Derby BISCUIT, inspiration of the later PARIAN WARE. Derby landscapes are famous, as are the 'Japan' patterns.

Marks range from the usual hopeful imitations of CHELSEA, MEISSEN, SEVRES, etc., to variations of the celebrated 'D', the crossed batons and the crown. The term 'Crown Derby' is usually applied to the period 1786 to 1811, and 'Bloor Derby' from then until 1848. It is to be noted that the present Royal Crown Derby Porcelain Company, which came into existence in 1876, uses the crown on its mark over a monogram of crossed 'D's'. This ware is generally called 'Royal Crown Derby'.

Door Knockers

Every day one sees more and more houses being pulled down to make way for new buildings. What happens to all their door knockers?

A great many eventually find their way into the

Dolphin door knocker

'Punch' door porter

junk and antique shops, and it is well worth treating yourself to a set for your own house. Once the Americans get hold of them they will never hang on English doors again.

They range from massive cast-iron ones, with a great ring in the mouth of, perhaps, a gargoyle or a lion, to more delicate efforts in brass (dolphins were a favourite symbol) or bronzed iron, and they can often be dated and traced to a manufacturer by the registry mark (p. 251).

Ornamental foot-scrapers are worth looking for, also old letter boxes and door knobs. This is a quest which will take you to the local scrapyard – which you should never pass without looking into.

Door Porters
Not, as you might think, men who carry doors on their backs, but articles of cast-iron, brass, glass and other materials used to prop open a door.

These survivals of an age in which, apparently, doors were kept open more than they are now, come in wonderful variety, and they are disappearing with great speed, most of them, it seems, to the United States and Canada.

But if we do want to prop open our doors in the evenings again and sing songs, as Chesterton recommended us to, there are still some stops about to do it with. All through the Victorian age the ironfounders, eager to show off their mastery of new skills in cast-iron, turned out by the hundred thousand all those replicas of Punch and Judy, the Duke of Wellington, Ally Sloper, Highlanders, bells, lions and other beasts. Usually there is some part of the figure which can be used to pick up the stop and drop it elsewhere, like the cocked hat of the Duke, or Mr Punch's curved bonnet.

You could make a fascinating collection of these for the garden (see GARDEN FURNITURE), painted against the weather. If you kept them indoors you could always 'blacklead' them and give your visitors a nostalgic glimpse of that unique sheen which long-departed charladies once gave our ironwork.

Other stops come in brass, cast in designs which have been made continuously for a couple of centuries, sometimes weighted with lead, sometimes not.

Then there are the green glass ones which are

Doulton stoneware jug

Hannah Barlow jug

properly a type of 'NAILSEA', with dew-beaded petals cunningly fixed inside them by the art of the glass-blower. These are fetching money nowadays. But the song of the revivalist is in the land here too, so be careful you aren't buying modern Birmingham. Unless, of course, you don't mind. They're nice things anyway.

Doulton

Although this firm has produced some fine stuff in its time – and still does – many of its Victorian wares rely on qualities still not entirely acceptable to us moderns. Their STONEWARE SPIRIT FLASKS are referred to elsewhere: just as fine are the many traditional jugs and bottles decorated in relief. Also in STONEWARE come the many jugs and vases with applied or incised decoration which, when the colours aren't either too drab or too gaudy, are fine things to have. There is a particularly attractive pale blue which sets off darker colours well.

Very much a personal favourite with me is the work of Hannah Barlow, who did some fine, economical drawings of animals in the stoneware while it was still soft, then rubbed pigments into the lines. Each of these is an individual piece of handwork, and I cannot see that they will fall below the 50s. to 60s. a piece which was being asked for them in 1960.

But there were many other fine artists at Doultons, and their work needs looking over and getting to-gether – as the museums are beginning to do. One thing that lends interest to Doulton collecting is that not only do pieces bear the firm's mark, but also the signatures or initials of individual artists.

Dresden

There have probably been more broken hearts about 'Dresden' than any other kind of porcelain, for none other has been so much imitated, forged, travestied and lied about during the last two hundred years.

Let's start by trying to get our terms sorted out. One is often asked the difference between 'DRESDEN' and 'MEISSEN'. To explain this we have to make a short excursion into history. PORCELAIN (HARD PASTE) was re-invented in Saxony about 1710 by a young German alchemist called Böttger. He had been locked up in a castle by the Elector Augustus the Strong until he could find the secret of making gold, and so help to pay for the enormous quantities of CHINESE PORCELAIN which Augustus had been buying out of his subjects' pockets. But Böttger discovered the secret of porcelain instead, which, from the Elector's point of view, was just as good.

From this sprung the Royal Porcelain Manufactory at Meissen, about twelve miles outside Dresden. Here were made all those entrancing figures of characters from the Italian Comedy by the famous modeller Kaendler and others which can cost you several

Dresden shepherdess

thousand pounds apiece; the famous CHINOISERIES, the beautiful little landscapes and seascapes in reversed panels on the celebrated grounds of yellow, green, lilac and maroon which were to be the inspiration of so much of the work of our own factories.

During the nineteenth century, however, not only did the Royal factory go on reproducing its own earlier wares in less refined forms, but outside factories, principally around Dresden, and also elsewhere in Europe, joined in the fun too. The result was the export of the huge quantities of 'Dresden' shepherdesses and other figures which filled Victorian mantelpieces and cases.

Not only were the famous crossed swords imitated, sometimes with qualifying initials (like 'S' for Samson) and sometimes not, but one firm even used one of the very early marks, 'A.R.' the monogram of Augustus the Strong. A crown over the letter 'D', also the word 'Dresden' itself, may indicate manufacture at, in or around Dresden, but it has nothing whatever to do with the work of the Royal Factory.

So there we are: 'Dresden', if you like, for all this secondary ware and imitations of the real thing. But if your own piece is to qualify as a rarity, it must be from the Royal factory, with the genuine mark; in which case you might as well follow the growing practice among serious collectors of calling it MEISSEN.

While still in Central Europe it might be worth mentioning the work of Berlin and Vienna, both of which had a distinguished early history like Meissen's, and both of which fell into similar habits of repeating their early successes. Berlin has continued down to the present day, though the old 'K.P.M.' (for Royal Porcelain Factory) has doubtless now changed itself into something more democratic. If you see the old shield (the *bindenschild*) of Austria on a piece in a junk shop the chances are that it was made after the factory closed in 1864, but is hoping to cash in on Vienna's ancient glory.

Dumb Waiter

Not what it sounds like, but one of those round, two- or three-tiered contrivances on pedestal feet used as a kind of sideboard, often revolving so that you won't have to walk round it to get the cheese or the decanter of port.

Two-tiered dumb waiter

Useful things, these, for one of those cocktail parties where you have to hold a glass in one hand, a sardine on toast in the other, and a cigarette in your mouth.

But wouldn't they look even better at a real party, decked out with flowers, jellies, sweetmeats (see GLASS TABLE) and other delights? And if the polish were stained by generations of spilt sauces and alcohol, you wouldn't have any sort of bad conscience about painting it up gaily in white, would you?

Earthenware

Here is the basic pot, dating from the moment when man discovered how useful clay receptables could be for holding water, cooking food, and, much later, putting flowers in.

At first he made a sort of wicker basket, plastered the sides with clay, then baked it hard in an oven. Later, he thought of the potter's wheel, whereby you could shape a lump of clay into any kind of a cup, plate or bowl merely by working a treadle with your foot and holding the revolving piece between your fingers. Then he found that it could also be cast in moulds, so it did not necessarily have to be round.

To hold water, earthenware needs a GLAZE, in other words a thin coating of glass, and this can be transparent, as on a WILLOW PATTERN plate or on the lower half of your bread-pan, or it can be coloured, like that gay vase on your mantelpiece. Alternatively, it can be covered with a thin 'batter' of clay, in which case it becomes SLIPWARE. Those interested in earthenware of various kinds could refer to 'BLUE AND WHITE', CHILDREN'S PLATES, CREAMWARE, DELFTWARE, 'MAJOLICA', MOCHA WARE, STAFFORDSHIRE PRINTED EARTHENWARE, SWANSEA, ETC.

Embroidery

I was only saying to myself the other day that one
didn't often come across old embroidery surviving in
a really satisfactory state when I saw six fine pieces
of Victorian Berlin work knocked down at an auction
for thirty shillings the lot, *including* two oil paintings.

I don't know how attractive Berlin work is to
modern tastes, but it was a real sensation in its day.

Embroidery, in general, of course, has been with
us for many a century, but it took an industrial-
minded nineteenth century to make things more or
less automatic with mass-produced cross-stitch designs, showing flowers, dogs, cats, birds, horses, deer.
On pieces of square-meshed canvas busy fingers
young and old occupied themselves all through the
long evenings, making firescreens, stool covers, backs
of chairs, slippers, even smoking caps and braces for
papa. They picked up the name from the Berlin
print-seller who introduced them to this country.

Later on, and very difficult to come across now, is
the more original art needlework to which ladies re-
acted later in the century. Outline patterns were
used, but there was room for considerable skill from
the needlewoman, and some of these end-of-the-
century designs of flowers and storks and peacocks
were very fine. One small item you often find in little
piles are the linen 'tidies' with which grandmama
kept her furniture clean from sticky fingers, or laid on
her sideboards and occasional tables.

Embroidered Pictures

These are rather a special sort of EMBROIDERY – and
by the same token rather a special sort of picture. I
suppose the sort one sees most are those rather lugu-
brious mourning pictures, showing a lady leaning on

a tomb, or perhaps a biblical scene, with Rebecca at the Well. Many of these were worked in silk which has now faded, or the background crumbled away with time. But there *are* attractive ones: I bought a handsome one some years ago, of a large peacock sitting on a small tree, for, I think, a couple of pounds. It was in reasonably good order, but I believe there are ways of rejuvenating these pictures, either by simply cleaning up or by giving a new background. Here is a chance for the really accomplished needle-woman to see what she can do by drawing in a few threads of bright colour to enliven the old.

Sailor's picture in wool

More primitive, of course, are all those sailors' pictures in wool, often of their own ships, or showing harbour scenes. Samplers belong to this school: I am not myself an enthusiast, for they so often express sentiments and interests imposed on a child by rather sententious parents. However, there they are, and many of them give a posthumous fame to some little lady of eight or nine.

'The Good Old Days'

My own favourite among all these things – and they have trebled in value over the past few years – are the small silk pictures machine-woven by a firm called Stevens.

It seems astonishing that pictures should be machine-made right in the middle of the nineteenth century, but I believe the process was simply an adaptation of the jacquard principle, which mechanized weaving generally. Anyway, the result of it all is a very lively series of small pictures in (when they are well preserved) astonishingly fresh-looking colours.

I first saw one of them in a very junky furniture store in Wednesbury – It was 'The Good Old Days', a fine little view of a mail coach bowling along with a full load. Oddly enough there was an exact duplicate in the shop as well, but as they were identical and not a pair – i.e. the coaches were driving the same way – I remained content with buying one for thirty shillings instead of the two for two pounds. I have since regretted this as much as afterward parting for three pounds with the one I *did* buy.

'The Present Time' is apparently the pair to 'The Good Old Days' and it shows a 'Puffing Billy'. Then there is 'The Last Lap', showing a flock of cyclists racing on penny farthings, and a whole lot of other scenes of the day, which you now see making their fivers and more. There are little book-marks too, I'm told, but I've never come across any.

Empire

In my rule-of-thumb way I tend to translate this term as 'Regency'; and while any expert can shoot large holes in this definition, it is probably near enough so far as the junk shop is concerned. In fact, you often hear people refer to certain kinds of Regency as 'English Empire'.

Outstanding feature of this style is the way it tried to copy the forms of Greece and Rome and in fact any ancient civilisation which happened to be in the news. For example, Napoleon's adventures in Egypt and Syria let loose a whole family of Egyptian designs, while soon afterwards our own forays into the Far East induced another outbreak of CHINOISERIES, including a few ideas from India and Persia.

Although these motifs quietened down after about 1830 it is surprising how traces of them lingered on right through to the end of the Victorian era. A good many of these things are in the junk shops still. For ten shillings I bought one of those double-ended 'Grecian' sofas in 'vicarage' pine, with classical scrolls on each arm: it also had Elizabethan 'bulb' legs thrown in for good measure. Tucked away in the back of a warehouse I found a splendid mahogany X-legged chair, direct from ancient Rome.

Pottery, metal-work, fabrics and every sort of bric-à-brac of the time reflected 'Empire'; and you could have a lot of fun gathering together examples of these English adaptations of exotic fancies.

Enamels

Enamel is really only a form of coloured glass applied to metal in the form of moistened powder. It has been

F

made for a very long time now, and there are several
methods of using it. The well-known 'BATTERSEA'
enamels (which as pointed out elsewhere are much
more likely to have come from Bilston) are perhaps
the best-known form in this country. But you will also
find a great many Chinese enamels, usually named
after CANTON, where a great deal of the work was
produced. Much of it was made by the method known
as *Cloisonné*, in which the enamel was placed inside
little 'cloisons' or walls, of metal, which separated
different colours. When the pattern is applied in little
pits or depressions, the term is *Champlevé*, while if the
whole surface is covered the work is spoken of as
encrusted.

For one of those reasons nobody can ever explain,
Canton enamels, which had been lurking here un-
loved since they were imported several generations
ago, were suddenly 'wanted' a few years ago, and a
surprising number appeared in the shops. I don't
know where they have gone – probably to America
or Italy.

One ought also, perhaps, to mention Limoges

Martinware face jug

enamels – although they are now museum pieces – in which the magnificent decoration was *en grisaille*, or in various tones of grey. And nothing whatever to do with 'Limoges' ware porcelain or pottery, either from France or from England.

Face Mugs and Jugs

Close relatives of the TOBY JUG, but concentrating on the face rather than the whole figure. The satyr's head is often seen, together with national heroes, notorieties, characters in fiction and legend. Many were made in Victorian days and later by firms like Doultons; in some cases they are still being made today.

Faience

This is the French version of our DELFTWARE and the Italian MAIOLICA, i.e. earthenware covered with an opaque tin glaze. It was made from the sixteenth century down to early nineteenth.

A late eighteenth-century tureen with shell edging, or a plate with the delightful French CHINOISERIES of Moustier or Marseilles will give you endless delight, but you will be lucky to find them in this country at all, let alone cheaply, for here they had to meet the strenuous competition of CREAMWARE.

The term *'faience'* was also most misleadingly used in the nineteenth century by potters like MINTONS and DOULTONS to describe a large class of pottery, covered with thick, coloured glazes, and with excellent qualities of its own – and therefore worthy of a name of its own, say I!

Fans

'I have seen a fan so very angry,' wrote Addison, 'that

18th-century painted fan

it would have been dangerous for the absent lover who provoked it to have come within the wave of it; and at other times I have seen it so very languishing that I have been glad for the lady's sake that the lover was at a sufficient distance from it.'

In days when tender conversation often had to take place across a room or from one theatre box to another, there was, it seems, a recognized code of signals, rather like semaphore. Collectors, of course, go for the now rare eighteenth-century fans, either those in which you inserted the latest paper song or political rhyme, or brisé fans, with their sticks joined by ribbons. But these are rare now, and we shall have to content ourselves with the painted ones of the Victorian age, or those large black Spanish ones in ebony.

Who knows, one day they may be used again for that 'infinite variety of motions in the flutter of a fan' of which the Spectator wrote. I can think of no better distraction from atom-bomb neurosis.

Firebacks

Our ancestors knew a thing or two about making the most of an open fire. Here and there you will come across one of the old cast-iron firebacks, taken from an old house which has been pulled down. It stood at the back of an open fireplace, partly to protect the bricks at the back from the heat, and partly to throw that heat out into the room – where it was wanted. In other words, to act as a sort of radiator. Another advantage it had was that once a thick slab of cast iron gets really hot, it keeps hot for a long time; and a fireback would keep a glow in your cheeks long after a fire had died away.

Added to all this, it gave you one more chance to show off your family arms or loyalties. For most of these backs have designs of one sort or another cast into them. A great many are heraldic, often bearing the arms of a specific family. Others feature Biblical subjects like Adam and Eve, or commemorate some public event, such as a coronation or a victory. The Boscobel Oak, with its three crowns in a tree, symbolizing the escape of the future Charles II, is a favourite device.

Prices for these firebacks seem to vary between £10 and £80, according to their elaboration and size; and if you think that a lot of money, remember that these firebacks last as long as a house does – longer, as we have seen.

At least, some of them have. For one of the odd things about these firebacks is that there is apparently an inexhaustible supply of them. I know at least one country antique shop, where one unfailingly sees a dozen or more, always with the same sort of patterns, and I'm sure these have never been inside a house at all.

Making new ones, of course, is simplicity itself: you use an old one to make your mould in sand, then cast a new one from it. The more battered and scorched the old one the better, for it will all register faithfully on the new one.

Experts can tell the true from the false by examination of the rust or patina. But non-experts will have to trust the dealer: after all, if he's an honest man, he ought to be able to tell you where it came from. If, of course, you mind. A fireback, after all, is a fireback and it's just as effective and decorative if it was cast yesterday or three hundred years ago.

Fireplace Furniture

A few years ago you could hardly give away old sets of fire-irons. Now you see them displayed on the walls of country cottages like warming-pans or old weapons. But fire-irons apart, there are many items which once stood in and around our fireplaces, and which, if unsuitable for collection, have something as decoration.

Having started at the back of the fire with FIRE-BACKS – and promising to go to the front of the fire with FIRESCREENS in the next piece – we could plump down halfway on *Firedogs*, which of course were made

Brass trivet

Fire dogs

to support logs so that they would burn freely on the open hearth. Many of these are still about, their uprights often showing cast figures, faces or initials, and still obtainable for a few pounds. A more stately version of this, made for show in the houses of the great, were the *Andirons*, sometimes of brass or even silver, beautifully worked, which stood at either end (thus 'endirons') of the fireplace and supported the fire-irons, especially after the introduction of the coal-burning grate.

Then there is all that range of smaller things from the hearth itself, like brass *Trivets*, to hang from the fire-bars, wrought-iron toasters, with sliding forks; and *Footmen*, to hold plates or dishes by the fire and keep them warm. There are *Smoker's Tongs*, with a spring in the handle, for lifting charcoal embers up to your pipe. *Smoke-jacks*, for turning spits, are occasionally seen.

If you heartily dislike your present grate, there are plenty of early ones worth looking at and not outrageously expensive, usually to be found in those junk

Fender

Helmet-shaped coal scuttle

shops which spread out around themselves in a yard. Don't be afraid of rust or breaks: there are still black-smiths about. Old *Fenders* are worth looking at too if you like workmanship better than that from the local multiple store. And for some other ideas about this old iron see GARDEN FURNITURE.

Fire Screens

In days when you had to warm a huge room with an equally huge fire, there was always the chance of getting scorched by it. Worse, perhaps, it could bring an unattractive glow to the face of your daughter – and that was no way to get her a wealthy and noble husband from among the gentlemen who came up from the dining-room.

So you provided yourself with a range of fire-screens. Sometimes they were full-sized ones, placed directly in front of the fire and called – for no very satisfactory reason that I can discover – cheval, or horse-screens. When it was desired to shield one particular part of the body – like that rosy cheek I mentioned – there

at those in the later Victorian BONE CHINA, in terra cotta, and in earthenwares like the MINTON 'MAJOLICA'. But before doing so, spare a glance for those fan-shaped affairs with five or six sockets for fixing on walls. The most delightful of them are in French FAIENCE, but the English PRATTWARE ones, with their hectic native colours, are worth having.

Furniture*

This really calls for a book on its own. But it may be worth while offering a few general remarks about the sort of things you may find in the not too expensive places. Only, the position is changing almost as one writes: pieces that to one's knowledge have hung about in warehouses for years suddenly disappear for a while, then turn up all nice and bright, in that exquisite little shop in the High Street.

But all the same it is still worth looking. Alongside the heavy Victoriana we hear so much about there

Bow-fronted chest of drawers

*For more about chairs, settees, tables and cupboards, see More Looking in Junk Shops.

Canterbury

are some pleasant pieces, designed originally for modest purposes, but still of good quality workmanship. So look very hard for such as the following:

Chests-of-drawers, which can be monstrosities, but can also be charming. I know one South London store where there are no fewer than four early-Victorian mahogany bow-fronted chests-of-drawers, at prices from £15 to about £30. You can put reproduction brass handles on the drawers, if you like, but they probably had knobs in the first place as they have now. The Victorians loved to show how rich they

Revolving bookcase

were by having all sorts of *Occasional tables*, and I would look at any which seemed to be a good shape and workmanship, whatever their condition so far as polish or paint or varnish was concerned. Then there was a great variety of *Canterburys*, used for music or magazines and newspapers, with sometimes a tray for your coffee and sandwiches at a dance. *Footstools*, too, come in a wide range, from long ones for the hearth rug, decorated in Berlin work or other needle-work, to small circular affairs on tiny mahogany feet. Now that we sit back and enjoy our television, these have come into their own again – and so are seen less and less frequently.

I mentioned under EMPIRE a Grecian style *Sofa* which I bought for 10s., but there are many other examples of this descendant of the daybed, as also *Settees*, which derive rather from a combination of chairs, sometimes being actually two-backed or three-backed; there are also wicker ones.

Chairs come in enormous profusion, although the

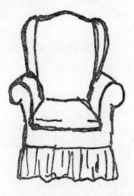

Wing chair

pleasant little upholstered *Sewing chairs* are getting hard to find, while anyone with any respect for their old age will buy up one of the deep *Wing chairs*. *Work-tables* and *Games tables* will hardly be found anywhere but in the dear shops, and *Whatnots*, especially the small ones, are mostly there too. But there are *Book-cases* in plenty, especially the sort which divide into two halves, glass above and cupboard below. Any amount of these are obtainable from four pounds upwards. Moderate sized *Chiffoniers* are not dear, and can be useful things in the small flat, while some of those ornate sideboards have high possibilities if you take off the back and strip off some of the bits of machine carving. In fact a great deal can be done by an amateur carpenter on some of the huge pieces, for undoubtedly this furniture is cheaper per square yard of wood than anything else he can buy today – or ever will. But he will have to go a great deal deeper into matters of cabinet-making and polishing than I can take him.

Two sorts of furniture, I think, are especially worth looking for. One is large old oak, which still hangs

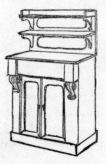

Chiffonier

Canterbury or magazine stand

about in spite of recent interest; the other is the much lighter style of things which broke out about the years 1890 to 1900. Some of these rather spare desks, tables and settees have quite a modern look; and I would have another look at *Art Nouveau*. Much criticised as it is, this was the only really original style evolved by the Victorians, and I would certainly sooner have a chair or settee of it in my hall than one of those great Abbotsford chairs, with all that barley sugar turning.

This is an absurdly inadequate survey of junk shop furniture, but as I said in the beginning, the subject

Invalid table

needs a book to itself – and somebody much more informed than I to write it. But there is just one other thought I would like to leave with you. Reports of sales at the big auctioneers' rooms can be entirely misleading so far as price is concerned. When you read that several thousand pounds were given for a Regency cabinet, or a set of Hepplewhite chairs, remember that at that same sale there was probably a pleasant little *Davenport*, or writing desk, a *Commode*, or some other piece of late Georgian furniture which went for less than the price of a modern settee. The reason seems to be that, to the sort of dealers who use these rooms, anything not in the top rank – 'important' as they say – is not of high interest, so it goes very reasonably. I know a person of very modest means who has furnished a London flat with genuine period things all bought at Sothebys.

For other items of furniture mentioned in the book see BAROMETERS, BUHL, CANDLESTANDS, CHINOISERIES, CHIPPENDALE, CLOCKS, DOOR KNOCKERS, DUMB WAITER, EMBROIDERED PICTURES, EMPIRE, FIREBACKS, FIREPLACE FURNITURE, FIRE SCREENS, GARDEN FURNITURE, GLASS PICTURES, HANGING SHELVES, HEPPLEWHITE, LAMPS, MARQUETRY, MIRRORS, ORMOLU, PAINTINGS AND PRINTS, PEMBROKE TABLE, PAPIER MÂCHÉ, PLAQUES, PONTYPOOL AND USK WARE, SHERATON, SILHOUETTES, SUTHERLAND TABLE, TEA CADDIES, ETC., TILES, TINSEL PICTURES, TUNBRIDGE WARE, WASH HAND STANDS, WAX FRUIT AND FLOWERS, WINDSOR CHAIRS, WORKBOXES.

Garden Furniture

Here's a happy hunting ground for a nation of gardeners. Why do we pay so much attention to flowers and so little to the many decorative things in metal, wood and stone which can beautify a garden.

Lath-sprung garden chair

Of course, the 'trade' have got on to this a long time ago, and they busily furbish up old park benches, offering them to you for a tenner or more. Sometimes, especially when the iron back is one of those wonderfully intricate castings which paint up so splendidly, they're well worth it, for nobody's likely to make them again.

But to show how one *can* pick up things let me tell you two little stories. One concerns myself. A couple of local boys had asked permission to build what they called a hide-out in my spinney, and one day I walked down to see what they were up to. Behind a high screen of brushwood I found a neat little tent, with pots and pans hanging from a framework of twigs, a camp fire and – of all things – one of those late Victorian iron garden chairs. With a boy in denims sitting in it, the whole scene looked rather like one of those pictures showing the *Times* war correspondent outside his tent at the Crimea.

But when I examined the chair I found it a fascinating piece of ingenuity. The circular seat was given a 'spring' by making it of laths arranged round a central boss like the spokes of a wheel: when you sat on it, the laths gave most gratefully.

I found that the boys had fished it out of an old rubbish pit nearby, and as they'd acquired it merely for the fun of doing so – boys never sit down for long anyway – they were delighted to part with it for a shilling. Since then I've looked up my chair in an old Harrods catalogue and there it is, part of a whole range of this furniture, priced 8s. 2d.

The other story harks back to that park bench I mentioned in the beginning. A neighbour was moving, and she left behind on the terrace a long bench, the legs of which were cast in the likeness of tree branches, a favourite form of Victorian decoration. But the thing was enormously heavy – those iron branches really *were* solid affairs – and as the wooden laths had rotted anyway nobody seemed to want it because of the sheer difficulty and cost of removing it.

But my old jobbing gardener walked up to it one day, smashed all the wood away leaving himself with three separate pieces of iron – the legs. He carried these away one at a time, got a carpenter to make him some more laths, joined up his three legs again, painted

Victorian bench with rustic legs

the iron branches a nice olive green and now flaunts
it outside his back door.

The country is, of course, the place to look for
things, for people there are apt to shove such things
away in their many outhouses and forget about them
until they have a sale. Then they're dragged out into
the light of day, spread over a field and you can really
pick things over. Look particularly for the things
mentioned under FIREPLACE FURNITURE: these often
have an application for the garden or for the small
yard. I once saw some very ornately pierced Victorian
fenders used for terracing a tiny garden, so enabling
the owner to garden vertically rather than horizon-
tally – which, as a non-gardener, I should have
thought a great help to backache. The terraces looked
nice, rather like a distant view of vineyards. I've also
seen one of those magnificent cast-iron stoves, covered
with intricate leaf patterns, built into the wall of a tiny
town courtyard, and not only giving the place tre-
mendous character, but wonderfully handy for keeping drinks cool in the summer.

Then there are all those urns that turn up whenever
a biggish house is pulled down – which is happening
all the time now, of course. Some of these are in
terra cotta, some in glazed earthenware or one of
the softer stones. You can buy new earthenware ones,
of course, and also concrete imitations of the stone ones,
but personally I'd rather go for the older ones. Ten
pounds will buy you something quite attractive, and
if that sounds a lot, think what you spend in seeds
over only a few years.

No doubt you will have seen the stone balustrading
and parapets along the roofs or on the terraces of big
houses: did you know that you can get this re-erected
in your garden at not a wildly impossible cost?

Going round the backs of public houses may not appeal to everybody but twice I've found there one of those old sandstone sinks they once used for cleaning pewter pots in. They make lovely miniature gardens, or bird baths, especially as they've got a plug hole for water; and being so weathered and worn, they've double the character of anything newly 'rustic'.

Staddle stones, for standing under a rick or granary to keep out rats and damp, have been sought for years now, and I suppose fresh ones will appear only when they pull down more granaries. But those old granite corner stones, used to deflect cartwheels as they turned sharply, might be obtainable if you talked nicely to the farmer, who now drives his Rover. In fact, *all* weathered and handworked stone is worth picking up.

Blacksmith's shops, such as are left – and there are more of them than you might think – are worth haunting. People used to take things there for repair, then forget about them, or the blacksmith would break them up for bits and pieces. I once found on a heap one of those ironwork flower stands which used to stand in conservatories, needing no more repair than could be done with a welding outfit: you see them painted up and offered for sale outside town antique shops at high prices. Also it's always worth poking about with a stick in the gardens of old cottage sites; you never know what you may find there, from an old lock (which one friend of mine sold to a collector) to a fine pewter tankard, or some old railings.

But if you want to see old garden furniture on the grand scale you ought to visit that quite unique four or five acres of walled garden in Isleworth, Middlesex, where the firm of Crowther operates. Here you will find enormous wrought-iron gates, delicate little

Iron plant stand

wellheads, statues, baronial fireplaces of marble standing out in the open air, lead cisterns and drainpipes with heraldic designs, stone balustrading, street lamps, pavilions, as well as sheds full of pieces of metal, stone and wood of every kind. Nobody minds your looking round – you simply push open a little wicket gate – and if you don't get scared at coming face to face with Nero or Caligula as you go through the trees, you can stay there for hours.

Glass

Once upon a time, so the legend goes, some Phoenician merchants were camping on a sandy shore in Syria and used some lumps of stone to support their cooking pots. The stone happened to be a carbonate of lime, and when the merchants had finished their meal they found that the sand under the ashes of the fire had melted into glass.

Whatever the truth of this particular legend, it was in some such way as this that glass was originally discovered, and it explains why comparatively undeveloped countries have always been able to produce quite sophisticated glass. For instance, excellent bottle glass, comparable with the English product, was being made in America while the first settlers were carving themselves a home out of the aboriginal forest among hostile Red Indians.

The whole story of glass, from the times of ancient Egypt, Syria, Rome and Islam down to the exquisite creations of Venice, also the Netherlandish, Bohemian and English contributions, can be studied in museums. You can also buy representative pieces of some of these in the salerooms – at a price. But even if you stay with English crystal, to limit oneself to a pound or two is to limit oneself indeed. After all, if we want a Georgian cut-glass bowl which has given pleasure to several generations before us, will live with us for our natural lives, and then have to get used to the company of those who succeed us, we ought not to grudge the dealer his ten or fifteen pounds.

But there is still a good deal of post-Georgian glass which will undoubtedly get dearer, and can be just as interesting to collect. For alongside all their extravagances the Victorians made excellent stuff. Furthermore, much of this is still inadequately documented, and the new collector will find here some of that fun of working in relatively uncharted seas mentioned in the introduction to this book.

So rather than attempt a survey of the whole subject of glass, which is quite outside the scope of the book, the following sections, and those to which cross-reference is made, simply draw attention to some collectable items of Georgian and later glass. Those with more serious intentions will go first to the standard works mentioned in the Reading List, then, for the later things, to trade periodicals, to the collectors – and to the junk shops.

Cut-glass vase

Glass (Flint, Lead or Crystal)

This is England's main contribution to glassmaking, a metal of exceptional beauty and clarity, designed to make the utmost use of the light falling upon it. At the moment it seems to be eclipsed in public interest by the more exotic GLASS (OPAQUE AND COLOURED), but if you can get out of your head the idea of colour and other fancy tricks – fascinating though some of these are – and concentrate on the particular beauty of clear glass, there are still many rewards to be won.

This sort of glass can be *blown*, either freely, in the spectacular way that always fascinates a visitor to a glasshouse, or in moulds. It can be *cut* on the wheel, either deeply or lightly, so as to present as many different surfaces as possible and so reveal its internal brilliance. It can be *engraved* with a sharp pointed tool in all manner of intriguing ways. It can be *etched* with acid in exactly the same way as an etching. It can be painted with enamels—otherwise, *enamelled*.

In finding your way about among these different types you will readily see the difference between the

Cut-glass tumbler

sharpness of the early cut-glass and the bluntness of the later *pressed* glass, while those blown in a mould will generally show the seam where the mould was opened to take out the pieces. This will sometimes have been filed away, and pressed pieces have been cut afterwards to make them look like cut-glass. Here you will find it necessary to study just what operations *can* be carried out by genuine cutting, for there is a limit to them – but none to the designs which can be pressed.

But don't despise pressed glass altogether. In its earlier forms, it still had a great deal of 'the hand-made' feel of old glass and these items are themselves becoming of interest now.

You have to be very eagle-eyed to come across many of the early sweetmeat glasses, jellies, and this applies also to other table wares, for example, cruet

Finger bowl

bottles, many of which can stand up quite stoutly as miniature works of art in their own right. When they have collars and lids of silver, they can be dated by the hallmark. Salts come boat-shaped, cup-shaped, some with feet like those in silver and pewter.

Finger bowls designed for fingers made sticky after exploring the sweetmeat bowls, are sought after nowadays and can be found plain, cut, moulded or otherwise decorated, also in BRISTOL blue and other colours. I have seen them set out on the table, each with a little candle floating on a raft in coloured water. They looked charming.

Of similar shape but with a little notch or two notches at the rim, are *wine-glass coolers*, which are sometimes taken for finger bowls. The notches are there so that you can hang your wine-glass in the water foot upwards to cool it until you are ready for the next wine. When you see these items in BRISTOL BLUE, with gilt decorations and at a low price, plonk down your money and depart as soon as possible.

These coolers take us naturally into the realm of *drinking glasses*. Almost all the early types are in the Sotheby class, and those in search of the famous *Jacobite glasses*, with their engraved allusions to the Stuart Pretenders, will know better than to look in this little

Opaque-twist wine glass

Victorian etched glass

book for information about them – or to seek them anywhere but among the specialist dealers. Even the *air-twist* and *opaque-twist* wines, which delight so many collectors with their slender white or coloured spirals, are expensive now, though not perhaps unduly so bearing in mind their scarcity and our fallen values. They weren't cheap even when new, for there was much intricate craftsmanship in the way the air-twist was evolved from a bubble of air, or a slender, twisted filament spun out of a sliver of opaque glass. But if you do go in for one or two, look out for the forgeries which clever people are putting into the shops.

Engraved and *etched* glasses in the earlier periods also make their price though, as mentioned, the late Victorian ones are due for more careful examination.

But just in case we are tempted to lay out a few pounds, and moving round the different shapes of glasses generally, we might start with the *Flutes*, which can be long or short – made for the very strong ales of those rumbustious days, a little of which went a very long way. The conical shape helped to trap the sediment and I have often wondered why these are not revived for some modern beers which rely on sediment for flavour.

Then there are the *Dwarf Ales* or *Thimbles* for even more virulent brews of stingo; and right at the other end of the scale the *Giant Ales*, or *Yards of Ales* often to be seen hanging above bars, a yard long and a real test for any drinker. A variation is dealt with under JOKE POTTERY AND GLASS.

Going back to the small fry again and passing this time to the spirits department, we have the *Drams*, short fubsy little glasses with large feet. Sometimes they have a corrugated bowl, so that you couldn't see how murky your liquor looked. Some of these were *Sham Drams*, with deceptively thick glass bottoms – useful if you want to keep your head when all about you are losing theirs, or alternatively, if you have the kind of guests who are always wanting re-fills.

Acclamation for toasts and the speeches that accompanied them was punctuated with enthusiastic use of *Firing Glasses*, which though short and fubsy like the drams, had feet so thick and solid that the gentlemen present could bang them on the table and make a noise like a volley of musket shots.

A real he-man's glass was the *Rummer*, alleged by some people to be named after the German *roemer*, by others after rum. The *roemer* school say they were too large for rum, which would have been taken in a dram, but perhaps they will have overlooked the need for a largish glass when drinking 'grog' – a mixture of rum, hot water and lemon well known to naval persons. It derives from that gallant Admiral Vernon, who was nicknamed 'old Grogram' after a cloak he favoured; the same sailor who gave the Staffordshire potters such a useful selling line when he captured Portobello.

Personally, I am very fond of another type of glass which has hitherto been despised by the serious collector, but has its fascination. These are known in the trade as 'pub wines', but perhaps we ought to call them *Tavern Glasses*, since they were by no means confined to wines. In a very heavy lead glass, full of bubbles and other pleasant little imperfections, often wildly out of shape, they obviously arose from a craftsman's need to produce something for everyday use, rather than an artist's conscious desire to please. They can be bought today at not much more than the cost of new glasses and having lasted several lifetimes already, they'll easily cope with yours – providing you don't hurl them on to a paved floor.

And if you have it in mind to give someone an inexpensive Christmas present (prices around 2s. 6d.– 5s.), buy them an old pickle jar, fill it with bath salts or sweets, tie a blue ribbon round it and stand by for an expensive box of chocolates in return.

GLASS DECANTERS are mentioned under that head.

Pickle jar

Ruby and flint vase and jug

Glass (Opaque and Coloured)

Here we move from the chaste delights of English
Lead or Flint into a world of ingenious tricks, the
more difficult and spectacular the better. But before
you get too fascinated with coloured and enamelled
glass let me warn you that other people like it just as
much as you do, and its charms are obvious, so you
mustn't ever expect to get it very cheaply. Even quite
late Victorian things, which you might have expected
to be lying around unconsidered, have long been
sought by pillaging Americans, who have a long
history of coloured glass of their own and consequently can't keep away from ours.

The aristocrat of our own species, in my view, is
that wonderful BRISTOL glass of the opaque white
eighteenth century, which many people mistake for
porcelain, being totally different from the various milk
or opaline glasses of later dates. But if the earlier
items are in the Sotheby class the later, on present
form, are not far behind them. Having said which,
let me inform you that in a shop selling reproduction
furniture, I recently bought a nice opaline vase,
beautifully impressed overall with a design of flowers,
for one pound.

Tinted-glass flower-vase

But moving on to Victorian coloured glass, the best place to see it in all its splendour is where most of it was made – at STOURBRIDGE. Here local rivalries will make you alternate between the entrance hall of the Stourbridge council offices and the Brierley Hill Library and Museum, where the helpful staff will tell you everything you want to know about the wonderful stuff they have in their cases. You will find examples of

Hand-painted milk glass vase

the well-known *Satin Glass*, whose name describes it, of *Spangled Glass* where flakes of gold and silver are encased in clear glass, *Spattered* or *Splashed* glass in a similar technique, *Cased Glass*, where an overlay of one colour is cut through to show other colours underneath. You ought also to look at GLASS (BRISTOL BLUE), NAILSEA, ROLLING PINS, GLASS TOYS, GLASS LUSTRE VASES, and SLAGWARE.

Hand-painted opaline vase

Glass (Bristol Blue)

Although a very great deal of blue (and also other coloured) glass was made in Bristol, 'Bristol Blue' is not so much an indication of the origin of the glass as of a particular kind of blue colouring matter. The name is said to derive from the fact that the characteristic radiant blue was due to the use of smalt imported from Saxony through Bristol.

What we *can* pin down to Bristol, however, are the

aforementioned and beautiful opaque-white glass-
wares painted in enamels by people like Michael
Edkins, mentioned on page 109.

Glass (Waterford)

The term 'Waterford', so often heard in the trade,
needs some explanation. Waterford glass can sometimes be identified either by an inscription, or by its
similarity to known pieces. But for the most part even
life-long experts can be puzzled to tell the difference
between Waterford (or any other Irish glass) and the
Stourbridge product of the same era.

For Irish glass of that time was made from much
the same materials and by the same workmen as
English, the industry having moved there simply to
avoid the heavy glass tax in England. The old story
about Waterford glass being identifiable by its blue
tinge is, it seems, a myth. But there *are* forgeries of
Waterford, which have been provided with this
fashionable tinge to take advantage of the legend, so
this should be suspected rather than welcomed.

In case all this damages a cherished piece in your
eyes, let me hasten to assure you that a piece of late
Georgian glass of the quality made at Waterford is just
as valuable wherever it was made and you're very
much to be envied for having it.

Glass Decanters

When you consider how much skill has gone into
their making, these are still surprisingly plentiful
today. I suppose few people bother to decant their
wines nowadays, preferring to take their spirits
directly from the bottle with labels on them.
Also one wouldn't want to collect a whole lot of
them.

Georgian decanters

All the same, people seem to be getting ideas about them, and all those very attractive ones you see priced at only a few pounds will disappear from the junk-shops.

You'll be lucky if you come across one of the early mallet-shaped decanters. It was these that succeeded the dark-glass SEALED BOTTLES on the tables of the gentry and bore round their necks the fascinating array of WINE LABELS which are so eagerly collected today. Then there were the barrel shapes, the 'tapers', the 'Rodneys' (seafaring ones these, with specially wide bottoms against the roll of the ship); square ones for travelling boxes taken on coach journeys, others with quatre-foil shoulders and so on down to those heavily cut things of the mid-Victorian era looking like prickly pears, which gave latter-day cut glass its rather unkind name of 'cut-and-slash'.

There's an interest, too, in the stoppers, the Gothick spire-finial, the disc and those fanciful ones in the shape of a heart: all of these have their meaning and interest to the student. I have also seen decanters which are divided into four compartments, each holding a different liquid and having its own spout.

H

Victorian claret jug and decanters

But look around for these things while they are still there and don't be too disturbed if they look cloudy: there are ways of cleaning them.

Glass Lustre Vases

No doubt it was the echo of a long-forgotten sermon, on some drowsy childhood afternoon, but for me the glass lustres which hung from vases on our sitting-room mantelpiece were always thought of as 'tinkling cymbals'. These icicle-like pendants certainly tinkled delightfully, or so it now seems: why did we lose our taste for this simple music?

No doubt these lustres (which, by the way, have no connection with LUSTRE WARE pottery) started in history simply as vases with scalloped rims, although their immediate ancestor may well have been the glass girandole of Georgian days, a sort of miniature candelabra also decorated with hanging glass prisms. At any rate, they become really fashionable at about the time of the Great Exhibition of 1851, first in the most splendid forms for the great houses, later in ordinary editions for the little people.

Today, the best ones are in overlay work, the white opaque outer casing being cut through decoratively to reveal coloured glass – ruby, amethyst-green and black – beneath. These are very pricey now but one sees the common sorts, in coloured opaque glass and painted with flowers, at no very outrageous price.

Victorian glass lustre vase

Glass Paperweights
Once upon a time these pretty items were a pleasant byway of collecting. But nowadays if you want to get together a few representative ones, you will have to go to the specialist dealers, or to the sale-rooms, where their prices make newspaper head-lines. Furthermore, they are being made again, very cheaply, and you will have to take some care not to find yourself paying top price for something out of the last consignment from Italy.

By far the most popular form of decoration is MILLEFIORI which means literally 'a thousand flowers'. Weights of this kind are made by arranging slender

Millefiori and sulphide paperweights

coloured glass rods into bundles in such a way that they form a pattern at the end when cut across. The glassmaker then fuses these rods into one, which is pulled out to great length by two men. It still keeps the original pattern just like a piece of Brighton Rock, and slices cut across this, all bearing the pattern, are then arranged in a 'stand' and covered in with a sphere of glass over the top.

Another kind of glass paperweight, which many prefer to *Millefiori*, is that in which posies of flowers, birds, fruits, butterflies, moths, etc. have been enshrined in the glass domes.

Some weights are in overlay technique, that is to say they have been made in clear glass as usual, then 'cased' with a layer of coloured glass, which is cut away in facets to provide little windows through which you can see the design. Of the same family, of course, is the 'Snowstorm' of our childhood days, which are now being made again, while a distant but very distinguished relative is the *cameo glass*, or sulphide, where little portraits, medallions and the object modelled in china clay are held inside clear glass.

Glass Pictures
There are two kinds of glass pictures. The more ambitious ones, popular in the eighteenth century, were actually *Mezzotints* (see PAINTINGS and PRINTS) mounted and coloured. The mezzotint was stuck face

downwards on a sheet of glass, and the actual paper removed from its back, thus leaving only the ink of the print remaining. Colouring was then applied over this by an intricate technique which often puzzles modern collectors, for the marks so made do not necessarily follow the forms of the picture on the front. Needless to say, all this was extremely skilled work, and some of the earlier specimens are very fine and make a price.

The second type of glass picture is a crude affair, almost a peasant art, but not without some charm, where a landscape has been directly painted on to the back of the glass in lively colours. Most of those I have seen show a castle or large house and a lake, often with a figure on the bank or a vessel sailing. Good specimens of this type with a curly maple frame can be bought for three to five pounds apiece and they often turn up in pairs.

Glass Toys

Once upon a time these delightful little items in plain, opaque and coloured glass were called 'friggers', for many of them were the spare-time product of a glass-blower 'frigging' about to earn himself the price of a drink from visitors to the glasshouse. Even today, if you go over a glass works, they will usually put on a show for you, blowing a long sausage of glass and making it explode with a report, or magically transforming a hot lump of treacly orange glass into a tiny duck, using nothing but a pair of tweezers.

But for many years now these things have been made on a full-time basis, probably in the same sort of small back-street workshop as those in the Potteries where so many STAFFORDSHIRE CHIMNEY ORNAMENTS were made. Only a year or so ago, while nosing around the Stourbridge area looking for coloured glass, I was directed to an outhouse at the back of an ordinary semi-detached cottage, where I found two men, father and son, in something about the size of a toolshed, making little sets of foxhounds and dogs, also ducks, swans, and other animals and birds. No elaborate equipment was needed. They each had a gas jet flaming out across a table away from them and they made up these tiny things by melting sticks of coloured glass in the flame and manipulating them into shape.

In Victorian days, these toys covered a far wider range than the glass menageries you see in the shops now. There were little trumpets and swords, BELLS, umbrellas, village pumps with buckets, walking sticks, tiny tobacco pipes, in fact anything which would be a challenge to the blower's skill and delight a customer. They seem to have been particularly fond of hats, for these come in all shapes and kinds, from bowlers to policemen's helmets. Some are in the form of salt cellars, others are inkwells or medicine bottles.

All these things are fetching their several pounds now, but I cannot help feeling that they deserve to. Nobody will ever design a machine to make such an entrancing variety of things, and also you will never again get anyone to make such things by hand so cheaply.

Glass toy hat

Glazes

Before EARTHENWARE will hold water you have to cover it with something, and the most effective material for this is a glaze, or a coating of glass, which can be transparent or coloured. This same device can be used also for decoration, as with the early lead-glaze figures made by Ralph Wood and others, or for both purposes, as with the opaque tin-enamel used in DELFTWARE, MAIOLICA and FAIENCE.

But these glazes, like that on PORCELAIN (SOFT PASTE) lie on the surface of the piece. They do not really become part of it, as does the glaze on PORCELAIN (HARD PASTE). Here the covering is of the same fusible rock as the piece itself, so they become united. This shows when you break a piece: you can't tell which is which. STONEWARE is also glazed, as described under SALTGLAZED STONEWARE.

Pieces can be decorated 'under the glaze', as with STAFFORDSHIRE PRINTED EARTHENWARE, and also NANKIN, when the glaze will protect the design for the life of the piece; or it can be put on 'over the glaze' and fired again to fix the decoration. Your finger will usually tell you the difference between these processes.

All this sounds rather technical, but in fact when you have found your way around among these different sorts of glazing and decorating methods you will begin to know quite a lot about the various categories of 'CHINA' and pottery.

Goss China

I suppose that, properly speaking, 'Goss' should go under SOUVENIR CHINA. It was usually as a souvenir of a seaside holiday or a stay with distant relatives that there came into Auntie Flo's cabinet those small pieces of 'ivory porcelain', bearing the arms of a town

Goss ware

or county and made in a world of different shapes –
shoes, houses, bottles, vases, etc.

But now that 'Goss' is being collected, it seems to
justify an entry of its own, especially as I notice that
it seems to be the products of William Henry Goss, of
Stoke-on-Trent, and not those of his competitors,
which are sought.

But it is still only shillings that are involved, so if
you happen to inherit Auntie Flo's cabinet, do not
yet go rushing off to Christie's or Sotheby's with it.

The Goss clan, who went on producing right down
to the 1920's, made other items which are being
looked at nowadays. One is called 'jewelled china', or
'jewelled porcelain' and consists of a very thin china
decorated with little 'jewels', or imitation emeralds,
rubies etc. made from enamels. Some of this was in
PARIAN ware. Goss also made a series of PARIAN
figures in a vein of late Victorian sentiment which
you have to like to be able to take. I saw a pair of
hunchback crossing-sweeper boys the other day at
seven pounds the pair. I'm afraid I'm *not* ready for
them yet, especially at that price!

Hanging Shelves

This is a piece of furniture which one often sees languishing unregarded in junk shops, high above one's head on a beam.

Perhaps people nowadays don't care to be bothered with the job of dusting things kept on open shelves. But I always think they seem to occupy so much less actual air space in a room than does a glass china cabinet or bookshelf. I saw a handsome pair the other day of the King William IV era, with open tracery sides, 'barley sugar' supports and a long, narrow drawer in the base. They didn't seem at all dear to me at £14 the pair.

Of course, if you want to spend more, there are much more glamorous ones than these, say in satin-wood, or with marquetry work on sides and front. You can also find quite handsome later ones; while if you move into the late Victorian era, there are those oriental-looking affairs in bamboo, with mirrors and little cabinets.

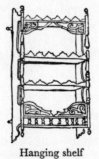

Hanging shelf

Hepplewhite

When someone shows you a piece of 'Hepplewhite' make sure you both realize that you are talking not

Hepplewhite chair

about its manufacturer, but about a style of furniture making.

George Hepplewhite, a London cabinet maker and upholsterer, who died in 1786, wrote the famous *Cabinet Maker and Upholsterer*, which helped the cabinet makers of the day to interpret Adam styles, promoted veneers and inlays and also curves. Typical were chairs with backs in shield, oval or heart shapes. It is now held, however, that these 'Hepplewhite' designs did not originate with him.

Horse Brasses

If the horse age has virtually passed, nobody can say the same for the age of the Horse Brass. If it had, this would certainly not be the fault of those modern brass-founders who assiduously supply a demand for brasses which is far higher today than when they were used on every farm, in every brewery, in dockyards, rail-way goods yards, in fact everywhere where heavy horses pulled loads and carters took a pride in their turnouts.

Some say that these brasses originated in the amulets worn in classical times to ward off the devil, just as a piece of moving tinfoil scares off rooks. In eighteenth-century England, the ancestor seems to have been the round sunflash, the simplest form of brass. By the middle of the nineteenth century, however, there were hundreds of different brasses, some of them very beautiful work indeed – horseshoes, acorns, flowers, lions, stags, swans, fox masks, portraits, bells, with trade devices like barrels for brewers, railway engines, ships.

Would-be collectors have to remember that these genuine brasses are nothing whatever to do with those sold in seaside shops as souvenirs, stamped out by the thousand. There are also fakes of the genuine old ones. To distinguish them, one must pay some attention to the feel and look of the older brass alloys and look for signs of wear from the constant rubbing of leather.

But why not also look at some other items of harness furniture where, so far as I know, the faker's hand has not yet appeared? These include those wonderful fly terrets or 'flyers' as they were called, with plumes of coloured horsehair, the rows of little

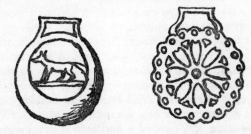

Horse brasses

BELLS, the brass hame plates, face pieces and other items.

Imari

A style of decoration in blue, red and gold perhaps most familiar to English collectors in MASONS' IRON-STONE. It took its name from the Japanese port for the pottery district of Arita, home of the KAKIEMON style.

As 'Brocaded Imari' it was the basis of the 'Japan' patterns used at WORCESTER, DERBY, SPODE and MINTONS. But in its day it has been badly manhandled and there are some pretty frightful versions of it in the junk shops. However, it cannot be denied that if you want something crude, colourful and tough, these later Imari STONE CHINAS certainly give you it.

Ivory

I have never been enormously attracted to ivory carving, perhaps because much of it is so painstakingly realistic. Being so perfect it's boring, rather like professional billiards. I've seen plaques with renaissance subjects at no very outrageous price, though I suspect that these were made long after the renaissance or they would be in Bond Street. Religious figures are said to hail largely from Dieppe.

Anyone who picks up a taste for Oriental mythology from CHINESE PORCELAIN will find much to interest them in the Chinese figures. Chessmen are a quarry for many people, and there is at least one specialist dealer in London who sells nothing else.

But for me ivory is most interesting where it has been used either as a decoration or in making some useful but attractive item for everyday use. The Victorians were very fond of it and used it in all sorts of ways – for such things as CARD CASES, paper knives, bodkin cases, cane handles, 'paper-thin' brooches, boxes and the rest. In jewellery, too, it had its day when highly coloured personal adornment went out in favour of 'plain' things like diamonds, JET and so on: there were many neck chains with huge carved links.

Another way of using it, of course, was as an inlay, for TEA CADDIES, WORK BOXES, various sorts of FURNITURE, including CLOCKS. Not many people realize, too, that the best portrait miniatures were usually painted on ivory.

The modest collector, sorting over the many things made of ivory or making use of it, could get together a charming and interesting collection at very reasonable cost.

Jackfield Ware

You will hear this name cheerfully applied to any earthenware (or china, for that matter) with a shiny, black glaze. It comes in many forms, notably teatable wares and figures, especially cows.

But as usual, there is 'Jackfield' and 'Jackfield' – this time we have to put *both* the words in quotes, because both are indications of a type rather than of origin in the Jackfield district of Shropshire.

What the general trade will show you as 'Jackfield' is typified by the two teapots I have, both in red earthenware covered by a shiny black glaze, which itself is very nearly covered by a mass of applied flower and leaf decorations in every colour of the rainbow, with gilding thrown in. You couldn't imagine anything more cottagey and Victorian – a sort of working man's version of COALPORT and ROCKINGHAM.

Ought this to be collected? I don't know, but somebody is buying it, for one teapot cost me 2s. 6d. while another, a couple of years later, cost me two pounds.

A sleek black cow, with a mended horn, cost 20s. in a street market.

I should certainly like to see a lot of it, if only out of curiosity to see what family groups it falls into.

As to the other 'Jackfield', this is very much collectors' ware, and in fact is not exactly black, but has a brownish or bronze tinge. It was made not only at Jackfield, but by celebrated early Staffordshire people like Whieldon. So you can see that here we are moving in pretty rarefied circles: it is serious pottery and has to be treated with the same sort of respect as, say, CREAMWARE.

As with BASALTES, some pieces on a white shelf can look as attractive as any other early ware of the kind.

Japanned Tin Ware

As production of this began in PONTYPOOL AND USK in the eighteenth century, it is mentioned under that head.

Jasper Ware

Here is what most people think of as WEDGWOOD. It has been a great favourite for nearly two centuries now, and there must be few houses which have not at least one small piece of Jasper ware somewhere. Of course it was not Josiah Wedgwood's only achievement in ceramics (see WEDGWOOD) and in many people's view far from being the most important; also, of course, many other potters besides Wedgwood made it.

Jasper ware is a fine stoneware, stained on the surface or throughout its body with the famous tints of blue, lavender, sage, lilac etc., and ornamented with applied relief decorations in white, mainly in classical styles.

Wedgwood went to enormous pains to find a suitable formula, and named it after the precious stone.

Jasper toilet pot

A success from the beginning, you can still see it being made today, by very much the same means as in Josiah's time, but in probably the most up-to-date pottery in the world.

Distinguishing between recent and older jasper isn't so easy, for most pieces simply bear the impressed mark WEDGWOOD. It is only really by close examination of the material and the quality of the relief moulding that you can tell: the earlier work has much greater depth and delicacy in the cutting.

One does not quite know where to begin in cataloguing the many kinds of things which have been made in Jasper ware. There are vases of all sorts, tea wares, medallions, candlesticks, trays, FLOWER and BULB POTS, chessmen, BUTTONS, PLAQUES, dishes, buckles, SCENT BOTTLES, PATCH BOXES, watch cases, CAMEOS on bracelets and brooches, chatelaines, combs, seals. You also find it in combination with glass, as for instance the drums on candelabra.

Other makers of Jasper ware included Humphrey Palmer, John TURNER, James Neale, William Adams and a few others. There are subtle differences in the work of these various potters. The blue on the Adams ware, for example, is more violet than Wedgwoods, while Turner's is a colder colour altogether.

Jet

Black isn't to everybody's taste, as we've already noted under BASALTES and JACKFIELD WARE, and you could hardly have anything blacker than jet. Yet most jewellery boxes have a piece or two of it, and to judge by the way modern manufacturers are imitating it in black glass or ebonite, it may well come back.

Jet hairpin

True jet – not to be confused with the sharply pointed 'French jet', or black glass, is a form of coal, and has been worked in Britain for ornaments since at least Roman times. It comes mainly from the Whitby area, where in Victorian times there were over two hundred workshops producing not only jewellery but small household articles as well, such as thimble cases, table vices, egg cups, paper knives etc.

Up to about 1850 jet as personal wear was largely associated with mourning, and for a very long time women presented at Court were allowed only jet jewellery. But when Queen Victoria's long period of mourning was over, there was an outbreak of highly coloured jewellery which, by a natural reaction, was followed by a vogue for things with more restraint –

Jet brooch

diamonds, ivory and jet. There were enormously long jet chains, with huge beads, also serpents of jet to be worn round the arms. Fair women must have looked magnificent in coronets made of jet beads.

Jewellery

This is so personal a thing that I don't know what one can usefully say about it. The smaller shops still have a great deal of inexpensive Victorian jewellery, of the sort that was made in vast quantities in those expanding times.

I think that here, as in so many other fields, the thing to look for is good and careful workmanship. There are exquisite little carvings in coral and ivory;

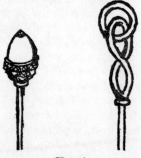

Hat pins

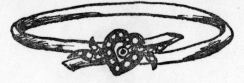

Gold bracelet with heart of pearls

there are the semi-precious stones like amethyst, onyx and the rest; there is cut-steel jewellery, cameos, SHELLWORK.

If it is a question of collecting rather than adorning, you could get together a little menagerie of dogs, horses, lions, snakes, butterflies, beetles, bees – even earwigs and bed-bugs! There were vogues for amber, jet and ivory necklaces of a huge size. Then there were the many brooches bearing names or mottoes, sporting items, like golf clubs, foxes' heads, horseshoes, with ships and anchors for sailors' wives – the catalogue is endless.

And all those hatpins! I suppose the ones with good stones have lost them long ago, but what of those with designs, like Prince of Wales Feathers, helmets, fans, with portrait medallions?

Scarf pins are worth looking for, our climate being what it is, and although perhaps the most often seen is the cameo, there are also those cast in the shape of an animal or some ornamental device, like the brooches mentioned above. Then, if you are very lucky, you may come across one of those painted ones, with portraits of well-known Victorian figures, or of dogs. These were real and actual dogs, and the portraits were painted from life by men like William Essex and William Bishop Ford, skilled miniature painters.

In fact, the thing to do is plunge into this vast store and see what you can find. Only, be very careful to examine what you buy for imperfections. Much of

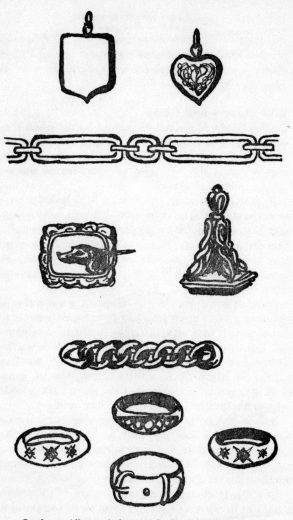

Lockets, Albert chain, scarf pin, pinchbeck seal, plaited gold brooch, **gipsy rings**

this stuff – though by no means all – is there because it's damaged, and therefore not worth buying. More about jewellery, especially gemstones, appears in *More Looking in Junk Shops*.

Joke Pottery and Glass

Our ancestors had some boisterous habits when they were at their ease in their inns. One of the things they never tired of doing was finding ways of taking the mickey out of their drinking companions by the use of joke mugs and glasses.

A favourite item in the family, which dates back to DELFTWARE times, is the fuddling cup, which consists of three or more cups joined together externally. You are asked to empty one of them, which seems an easy enough task. But the cups are also joined by secret channels, so that in emptying one you have to drain the lot.

Another is the puzzle jug. This has a whole lot of spouts and other apertures, and it seems impossible to drink out of it without spilling the liquid all over yourself. But there is usually a hole leading back down the handle, and if you stop up some of the spouts, you can get the liquid up through this channel, though sometimes you have to suck hard. One variety is a puzzle even to fill, for it has a hole through the bottom!

Still in the pottery world is the frog mug, which has a frog fixed near the bottom. As you empty the mug, not only does the frog appear and scare you out of your wits, but the air rushing through a small aperture makes a most lifelike gurgling sound.

In glass, of course, there is the 'yard of ale', with a bulb at the foot. It does not seem to be too formidable a job to empty one. But beware! there is a bulb at the end of the glass, and as you tip up the glass to drain the end of the beer, air rushes down into the bulb and squirts the stuff squarely into your face.

Another little pleasantry, reserved for newly married couples, was the marriage bell. This was a wooden affair, and was filled with wine or beer for the groom to toast the bride. But as the joker handed it over he pressed the handle and caused the wine to disappear into a receptacle at the top, thus leaving nothing for the groom to drink. (Discomfiture of happy couple, as Victorian *Punch* used to say.)

Kakiemon

A style of decoration originating at Arita in Japan, in which flowers, trees and figures are painted in enamels in typical Japanese asymmetrical designs in a bright palette of orange, green and pale blue. Named after a family of potters, it was much followed at MEISSEN and in the English PORCELAIN (SOFT PASTE) factories; and in fact I bought a little plate with the well-known 'partridge' pattern only a few years ago as a new WORCESTER production.

Knife Cases

You usually find these knife-boxes or cases with their insides pulled out and fitted up as stationery cabinets, with racks for writing paper and envelopes.

For this purpose, they're most practical and they can look very handsome in the centre of a writing table or desk. You can usually pick up a modest Regency one for about five pounds.

You may well wonder why people should have used such elegant containers for their knives, obviously intended as furniture for the dining-room rather than the kitchen. The point was that knives were a costly item in a household, and servants were not very

Eighteenth-century knife-boxes

highly paid. It was asking for trouble to let the knives go out to the scullions, so the footmen washed them in the dining-room, under the eagle eye of the butler, and then stuck them into the holes in these cases. You could see at a glance if any were missing by running your eye down the rows. Then they were locked – like TEA CADDIES – and the key kept in the pantry, or perhaps, on the reticule carried at the waist by the lady of the house.

Sometimes these cases are quite plain, sometimes of a wood like mahogany inlaid with other woods, or mounted with silver, showing, perhaps, a crest.

And there's another quite different shape. It's a huge affair like an urn, and you see these standing at either end of those long Georgian buffets, looking very classical and rather funereal. They are sometimes on pedestals which once contained tin-lined boxes for washing up the knives.

Candle lamp

Lamps (and Lanthorns)

A good-sized part of 'the trade' is involved in what it calls 'lamping', and many a fine and unique vase or figure has, to the fury of serious collectors, been immolated on the 'lamper's' bench.

Of course, there are plenty of things which *can* be 'lamped' without getting people into a bad temper, and not necessarily vases either. The other day I saw a pair of the famous Marly horses, not in BRONZE, of course, but in some cheap light alloy, which had been painted a shining white and given a bracket and nicely chosen shades. You can buy these for a couple of pounds or less – I bought one for seven and sixpence only the other day. You can also have 'lamping' fun with big chemical glass and STONEWARE.

As to lamps which started life as lamps, here is a fascinating study for someone. The big old houses of other days, with their many rooms and passages and staircases must have carried hundreds of lamps of various kinds, from the great candelabra in the drawing-rooms to the small lanterns with one or two candles to fix to walls of passages or to stand on tables at corners. Some seem to have a mirror plate, but no arrangements for a candle: these no doubt carried a glass or porcelain portable candlestick. The early ones are not easy to find – although this is a deficiency which modern coppersmiths are working hard, it seems, to fill! But there are still to be found the later table lamps, perhaps of brass, with globes of blown and frosted glass. These go for perhaps four pounds in the junk shops and eight in the decorators' shops.

Oddly enough, the Victorian manufacturers put more good taste and good sense into these than most of their wares. No doubt they enjoyed working under the restraint of a practical end. Watch out for the Argand lamp, with a reservoir for colza or other oil which feeds the lamp by gravity; these are very much sought after. And don't be discouraged if you find lamps that have lost their original shades; if you want a new 'original' glass one, the 'trade' can supply it!

Leeds
A famous name for CREAMWARE, q.v.

Liverpool
The Merseyside town has been a centre for the production of DELFTWARE and PORCELAIN, for the decoration of wares sent 'in the white' from potteries elsewhere (especially the 'Potteries') and for the productions of the Herculaneum factory (1793–1840). These latter include wares similar to STAFFORDSHIRE PRINTED EARTHENWARE, STONEWARE jugs, EARTHENWARE figures and NEW HALL type porcelain, sometimes bearing either the name of the pottery or a representation of the Liver Bird.

**Victorian standard lamp, brass argand table lamp,
hanging brass oil lamp and candle lamp**

Long Elizas

Outstanding examples of CHINOISERIES are the tall
Chinese ladies painted on PORCELAIN exported to
England in the eighteenth century; and imitated here
at places like BRISTOL, WORCESTER, etc.

The Chinese decorators evidently considered these
ladies very attractive – perhaps because most Chinese
ladies are short – and called them Mei-yen, or 'graceful ladies'. But the Dutch merchants who brought
these wares round the Cape of Good Hope did not
share this opinion, for they named them *Lange Lijzen*,
literally, 'long stupids'. The nearest our own people
could get to Lange Lijzen was 'Long Elizas' and that
is what they have been called ever since.

Longton Hall

An early PORCELAIN (SOFT PASTE) factory hopelessly
beyond our reach. The only reason I mention it is
that there is one Longton Hall type of ware, a rather
heavy white porcelain decorated with a 'wet' sort of
blue glaze which is so crude in appearance that it
could, just *could*, get itself mixed up with some third-
rate CHINA of similar shapes.

Lowestoft

It sometimes puzzles people to hear obvious CHINESE
PORCELAIN described as 'Lowestoft'. This all started
because a nineteenth-century ceramic writer called
Chaffers thought that these wares had been either
made or decorated in the Suffolk town: he had probably come across some pieces of Chinese ware which
imitated Lowestoft patterns – as the Chinese imitated
most patterns. Lowestoft was actually a SOFT PASTE
factory working between 1757 and 1802 in much the
same styles as BOW.

But the Chaffers name stuck, and the 'trade' still talks of 'Chinese Lowestoft', and when they refer to the many large dinner services which were made in China to the order of English families and decorated with their arms, you have 'Armorial Lowestoft', now very expensive. But note that some wares bearing coats of arms were made by SPODE and others in 'felspar porcelain', also 'STONE CHINA' and its variations, often as replacements in Chinese sets.

Lustre Ware

There are GLASS LUSTRE VASES (q.v.), with their tinkling icicles and there is also Lustre Ware, something quite different.

It is the name usually given to pottery, BONE CHINA and PORCELAIN which is decorated either partly, or wholly, with a shiny metallic glaze, sometimes pink or purple, sometimes silver or gold, sometimes copper.

In darkish rooms, lit only by candles or oil lamps, it must have gleamed most attractively from the

'Resist' lustre jug

mantelpiece, or on the crowded dresser. It has never lost its popularity and is still being made today, sometimes with new designs – Wedgwood have a very attractive jug – but sometimes in deliberate imitations of the old. It is getting dearer all the time, and the better pieces make high prices at auction.

Aristocrats of the family are the large silver 'resist' jugs, plain or with canary yellow and other coloured grounds. The 'silver' is really a thin coating of metal, not actually silver but platinum; and in the same way 'copper' lustre is obtained by using a solution of gold. The name 'resist' arises because of the way the lustre pattern is obtained. You paint it on to the white 'body' of the piece with a substance which will 'resist' or throw off any metal solution. When you dip the piece into this solution the part covered is thus left 'in the white'.

There is another type – also still being made – which is entirely covered with lustre, but personally I don't find these nearly so attractive, for they seem to me to be just aping silver or gold, as the case may be. I don't see why pottery should try to look like something else – what has it got to be ashamed of?

The most attractive of the older pieces, I think, apart from the resist patterns, are the big jugs with printed views or painted decoration, sometimes combined with relief work. These, too, are in the big money class but well worth it. The views of Sunderland Bridge are famous, and have given the name of this town to the whole class of ware, although it was made in many other places as well, especially Staffordshire.

There is also a whole family of wares with verses, pictures of lovers parting or meeting, to say nothing

Sunderland jug

of those PLAQUES which utter frightful warnings about
the next world. These usually feature that special
kind of purple lustre which was developed in the
Sunderland area with blotches and bubbles in it: this
was done by blowing oil on the glaze with a tube;
and it was thought very *chic* in its day.

I notice too that prices are steadily rising for the
ordinary tea-table items, decorated with lustre patterns. Some of this is most charmingly 'cottagy' and
it falls into several groups which have not yet been
properly sorted out. There is a whole family, for
example, which is painted with bold designs of a
church or house, another has sprigs of flowers in a
NEW HALL style and limits the lustre to borderings.
The quality of the paste varies very widely from a
crude earthenware to a very fine sort of china.

I have noticed that if you buy sets, or part sets, the
price at the moment seems to be about thirty shillings
to two pounds each, including, of course, teapot, jug,
large bowls and everything. But it doesn't stay in the
shops long, so once again, either get in on it quickly,
or leave it altogether.

Maiolica

So far as technique is concerned, this is the Italian equivalent of our DELFTWARE and the French FAIENCE – that is to say, earthenware covered with an opaque tin glaze. But it is totally different in treatment, characteristic subjects being historical or mythological scenes painted in brilliant colours and great detail. Mostly with the museums (the Victoria and Albert has what must be one of the finest collections in the world) and with the rich collectors.

'Majolica'

This word, thus spelt to distinguish it from MAIOLICA (it ought also to be in quotes to make the distinction even clearer) was the name given by MINTONS and others in the last century to describe an earthenware covered with a thick coloured glaze, which one still sees, not only on decorative vases and other wares but on the outsides of Victorian public-houses, in old-fashioned dairies, banks and even public lavatories.

Minton 'majolica'

Marble Glass
Sometimes known as Purple Slag and covered under
SLAGWARE.

Marquetry
You won't find a great deal of marquetry in the shops
unless it wants repairing, which is fairly costly. But it
might be useful to point out the difference between
marquetry and inlay, so that you can see what is
involved in the repairs. Inlaid wood is like any other
kind of inlay, being a piece of wood of one kind let
into a wood of another kind. But marquetry is a sort
of jigsaw veneer. Sheets of different coloured woods
are first glued together into a sort of 'sandwich', and
the design is cut through all the layers. Then the
sheets are taken apart again, and a jigsaw made up
by fitting the 'capes' in one coloured sheet into the
'bays' of another. Then all this is glued on to the
'carcase' of the piece, as with ordinary veneering.
And remember, that just as any sort of veneering likes
neither damp nor extreme heat, neither does marquetry.

Martinware
The stonewares produced by the Martin Brothers, of
Southall, Middlesex, towards the end of the Victorian
era are not everyone's cup of tea. Although some of
the vases and bottles have pleasant shapes and interesting textures, they are rather drab, I find.
As for the queer animals and birds, often with
rather unpleasant human faces, and the grotesque
MASK JUGS, these are not easy to fall in love with at
once.
    I only mention the ware at all, because it has found
its way into the Bond Street auction rooms, where it

Martinware jug

makes respectable prices. So if you have any of it, don't let it go for nothing.

Mary Gregory

Yes, there was a lady called Mary Gregory. But I'm afraid she didn't make much of the decorated glass which goes by her name.

You'll recognize these items from the drawing, I hope. On a whole range of decanters, jugs, glasses, bottles, boxes, flower holders and so on, you find figures of children painted in white or coloured enamels. Very decorous they are, these young people, in their long frocks or sailor suits, and they're usually picking flowers, blowing bubbles, flying kites or just walking along.

I have three before me as I write. One of them, a rather splendid green bottle with a high handle, shows a little girl standing rather precariously on the branch of a tree picking what appear to be peaches. Another, a quite ordinary green carafe, shows a boy about to bowl a hoop. In both these, the enamel decoration is of good quality and wholly in white. But in the third, which is a cheap clear carafe, the features of the little girl are given crudely painted flesh tints.

For years I had listened to tales of a dear old lady somewhere in the Stourbridge area buying clear-glass decanters and glasses from the local glasshouses and taking them home to her creeper-clad cottage, where she eked out a frugal living painting on them pictures of the dear little children who played outside her back door.

Well, something like this may have happened in the case of the tinted crude ones, no doubt made late in the last century or even after. But the early ones, in good glass and with finely judged white enamel painting, have a very different origin. They were made between 1850 and 1880 at Jablonec, in what is now Czechoslovakia, by a firm called Hahn, who

Mary Gregory jug

exported all kinds of decorated glass all over the world. This has been proved beyond all doubt by an American writer, Mr Carl W. Drepperd, who has come across a catalogue of the firm's products illustrated in colour and with all the pattern numbers.

And Mary Gregory? It seems that she was a lady who worked at the Boston and Sandwich Glass Works doing similar things to the Jablonec glass. And presumably *we* used the name 'Mary Gregory' because the American collectors of this glass asked for it here under that name. So do legends grow in collecting – and so are they destroyed!

Mason's Ironstone

Everybody will know the famous sets of octagonal jugs with snake handles which are almost the trade mark of Masons and their famous ironstone. It was a tough, practically indestructible earthenware aimed at the middle-class household of the early nineteenth century who liked their crockery to be as showy as the more expensive BONE CHINA, but wanted it to last twice as long.

Gathering a full set of the jugs would probably take a lifetime – though it would hardly cost a fortune. They came in sets, ranging from tiny ones a couple of inches high to giants standing 10 in. Mugs were also made, of course, and immense dinner services come up for auction and are eagerly bought by the trade, presumably for splitting up and selling separately.

Charles James Mason, who patented this famous ware, also turned out some huge pieces, vases five feet high, mantelpieces, baths, bedposts, and at least one whole fireplace. The firm of George L. Ashworth and Brothers, who bought the Mason's interests in

Mason's ironstone jug

1851, still make, among their more modern styles, reproductions of the original jugs.

Meissen
The products of the Royal Porcelain Factory at Meissen, Saxony, are discussed under DRESDEN.

Minster Jugs
A member of the APOSTLE JUG family and mentioned under that name.

Millefiori
Since millefiori glass occurs mainly in GLASS PAPER-WEIGHTS, this subject has been dealt with there.

Minton
One of the household names in English ceramics, of course, and still going strong. The founder, Thomas Minton, goes far enough back into potting history to

Minton chocolate cup and saucer

have had quite a lot to do with the popularity of the WILLOW PATTERN. Originally an engraver, he set up in business as a potter at Stoke-on-Trent in 1796, and the firm was greatly expanded by his son Herbert Minton (1793–1858), who became perhaps the leading figure in the whole industry.

At one time or another Mintons have produced pretty well every kind of ware and you could devote several lifetimes to collecting just a few of them. BLUE AND WHITE earthenware can be found marked with a floral cartouche and 'M. and Co.' or 'M. & H.' (from the Minton and Hollins period), while the Sèvres mark with an 'M' is famous. The well-known TILES, with decorations by Pugin and others can be found priced at a pound or cheaper.

In mid-Victorian times, the firm imported foreign artists and much fine painting was done in the styles of Sèvres, sometimes indistinguishable from the original work. (In a Sotheby catalogue not very long ago I saw a vase described as 'Sèvres or Minton'.) A leading part was played in the production of PARIAN WARE, the so-called 'MAJOLICA' glazed ware was

developed, while there were also highly specialized
items like the PÂTE-SUR-PÂTE decoration by M. L.
Solon, ornamental stoneware by Alfred Stevens and
others, also the extraordinary revivals of old French
Palissy Ware, with evil-looking snakes lurking at the
bottoms of dishes, a style later followed by potters in
Portugal, of all places, examples of which are often to
be found.

All this time the firm went on producing its
fine table wares; and still probably equips as many
bridal couples with household china as any other
potter.

Mirrors

I always think that if you can't afford large elegances,
it's worth giving a thought to small ones. A very
handy and comparatively inexpensive source of
Georgian or Regency elegance is the swinging mirror,
or toilet glass, as some people seem to prefer to call it.
Put one of these on a bow-fronted chest-of-drawers
and you somehow give the room a distinction which
would cost pounds to achieve in any other way.

These glasses come in all shapes, sometimes on
stands with a drawer, sometimes as simply an oval or
shield-shaped framework. Most good antique shops
will find you one and they turn up regularly at the
sales, sometimes going for as little as ten to fifteen
pounds.

Some people are inclined to be put off by seeing the
mirror itself in a poor state, but this is the easiest thing
to remedy: you can either have them re-silvered, or in
bad cases put in a new glass.

Another sort of mirror which is getting very popular
again is the small round convex one, which gives you a
complete view of the room. In other days the mistress

of the house liked to have one of these by the fireplace or wherever she habitually sat, so that she could see what the servants were up to behind her, or who was coming into the room. In combination with other mirrors they certainly opened up vistas all round and made the room seem large.

Talking of that, don't forget the proper purpose of a *Pier Glass*, which was to help light up a wall between windows. In the eighteenth century most rooms had windows along one side only, so that the 'pier' wall between the windows tended to be in shadow, too dark for a picture. So you put a long narrow mirror there and this not only reflected light from the opposite wall but as the light from outside fell directly upon people in the room, they could admire themselves in it.

And while still on the subject of pictures, don't overlook the possibilities of those old picture frames

Victorian shaving mirror

Victorian toilet glass

you see stacked away in the backs of shops, or sur-
rounding some frightful Victorian print or water
colour. You can often pick up very reasonably a curly
maple or gilded frame, which can be cut down to fit a
mirror. It will give you your small elegance very
cheaply indeed.

Mocha Ware

Most people know Mocha ware by sight, even if they
don't know it by that name. It's also called moss,
tree, seaweed or fern pottery.

Outstanding are the mugs and large jugs, with
bands of bright colours against a drab background,
and on every one is the characteristic feathery or
fernlike mark, like ink running on blotting paper – as
seen in Mocha stone, a kind of quartz.

People of no very great age will remember when
jugs and other table ware made of it could be found in
every kitchen, and cider and beer mugs in every
'local'. But none of it has been made for fifty years
now, so it has become an antique: moreover, one
which looks surprisingly at home among contemporary
styles.

Mocha jug

It was made in this country – and apparently nowhere else – for about 130 years up to 1914 and although that's well within living memory, it isn't generally agreed as to how the feathering effect was obtained. Probably different centres had different formulae but in all cases this decoration was put on while the pot was still wet from the potters' hands. A touch of a 'tea' made from tobacco, printer's ink and water was applied and this ran down and spread, looking like a crude sort of tree or fern. As well as the mugs and jugs, there are vases, doll's-house sets, ewers and other household items.

Some collectors go for the measures, which you will still see on shrimp and cockle stalls in street markets. Often these bear the excise mark, either in the form of an applied pad of clay or metal tag, and so are above reproach. But there is another race of them, with deceptively thick bottoms (and no excise marks!) which must have laid the foundations of many a modern shopkeeping fortune.

Although Mocha ware has been collected by a few interested people for a long time now, it's only lately become really fashionable. A very fine collection of it has been made by Noel Teulon-Porter, and the Stoke-on-Trent Museum, who will inherit this, has published a booklet about it.

Money Boxes

Once upon a time, when people saved their pennies more carefully than they do now, every chimney piece had its money box, a little earthenware container so cheap that it was smashed each year for its contents. There is good authority for believing that this was the origin of our term 'Christmas Box', dating from the days when apprentices used them.

But just because so many of them *were* broken in this way, they aren't very easy to find: so I could wish you no better luck than to come across one of the charming little boxes in the shape of fir-cones, pigs, hens, cradles, houses, chests-of-drawers and so on. They were made in most of the pottery centres, often

American mechanical penny bank

in brown 'Rockingham' glaze like that used for STONEWARE SPIRIT FLASKS. Serious collectors can sometimes pin them down to a particular factory or centre.

I notice the ones that do survive seem to have a pretty big aperture for the penny. No doubt in these cases, the money was extracted by adroit use of a knife as with the tin ones of our youth. Remember?

Moulds and Shapes

Difficult otherwise to describe all those wooden butter and gingerbread moulds, the latter with fantastic figures and other decorations – Punch and Judy, horses, shoes, bells, lovers' knots, pointed questions like 'Do you love me?' and even 'Will you marry me?'

You can also find earthenware jelly moulds of designs you don't see in the shops today. I found two creamware Wedgwood ones in a junk shed the other day among a lot of old tin cooking pans: sixpence each!

There are fine COPPER ones too. Definitely a quest for those who don't mind ferreting about at sales.

Butter moulds and sugar moulds

Nailsea flask

'Nailsea'

Here is another of those terms like BATTERSEA or JACKFIELD, which are misleading only if you accept them as 'guaranteed' indications of origin in a particular place. There are three or four types of glass known as 'Nailsea' in the trade, but probably far more of it was made in other centres like BRISTOL, Stourbridge, Birmingham, Newcastle, York etc., than ever came out of the Somerset village just outside Bristol.

Glassmaking at Nailsea seems to have started when a Bristol brewer founded a bottle factory there. Clear glass was heavily taxed during the Napoleonic wars and the factory hit on the bright idea of making decorative items out of the ordinary greeny-brown glass they used for bottles, which was taxed at only a fraction of the rate on clear glass. Hence all those dark-glass bottles with flecked decorations of coloured enamel glass, also the celebrated ROLLING PINS, flasks and other items, no doubt mainly sold as 'fairings' in markets.

Another sort of 'Nailsea' is typified by flasks in clear glass striped with pink or yellow in what is known as a *latticinio* style. People think this style was brought to Nailsea by French glassblowers imported by the owners of the factory. Then there are a whole range of things, some like those described under GLASS TOYS, other items such as a giant bellows, candlesticks, coaching horns, walking sticks, tobacco pipes, shepherds' crooks, and BELLS in various colours.

But remember that glassblowing skill is still about, and there is no doubt that many of the 'Nailsea' items you see have never themselves seen either Nailsea or the nineteenth century.

I am not myself sure that this matters much. There are some things which are so much 'of their period' that to fake them is a travesty, an error of taste as well as a swindle. But it seems to me that – for example – those dark bottles with coloured flecks are not particularly of any period at all. If you doubt this, put one of them among some modern fabrics – it could be the latest import from Italy.

So I don't mind 'Nailsea' fakes: in fact, at the risk of brickbats from serious collectors I'd say it's a pity they're not more readily available.

Nankin

Everyone will know the large oblong tureens in 'BLUE AND WHITE' CHINESE PORCELAIN with rounded corners, and a large bud knop, often found *en suite* with a service of massive plates and dishes. The trade calls this 'Nankin', and it came here in vast quantities through the eighteenth and early nineteenth centuries from the Chinese port of that name, where there were many decorating shops.

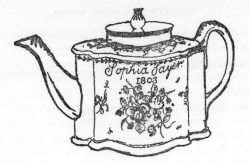

New Hall teapot

New Hall

Here is a CHINA, some of it a PORCELAIN (HARD PASTE)
which has always seemed to me the Cinderella of
them all, and in possibly two senses.

First, it was just a little old-fashioned even when it
was made – between 1782 and 1825 – and doesn't it
look it when you put it alongside the sophisticated
wares of contemporary Derby and Worcester? Buyers
of this ware were the provincial middle-classes, who
liked the simple charming sprigs of flowers and landscapes, who still drank their tea from the saucers, and
so clung to the little handle-less bowls fashionable in
Mayfair a generation before; and who liked their
teapots and jugs to at least have the shapes of silver
even if they couldn't always be made of it. You
can spot those teapots and jugs from the top of a
bus.

My second reason for regarding New Hall as a
Cinderella is that prices for it are not outrageous even
now. In 1958 I saw a teapot like the one shown, though
without an inscription, and having only a tiny chip
(which I didn't even see until the dealer pointed it
out) priced at £2 15s. A cup and saucer often goes

for 25s. and a jug is perhaps a little dearer. I bought a tea bowl in a 'china' shop for a shilling.

Considering that New Hall occupies quite a historic position – it inherited the patent of William Cookworthy, the Englishman who re-invented PORCELAIN (HARD PASTE) – these prices aren't high.

Note, however, that it was made in BONE CHINA as well as in porcelain, the former usually having 'New Hall' printed inside a double circle, the latter a pattern number. Note also that similar wares were made by MASONS of IRONSTONE fame, DAVENPORT, MINTON, Chamberlains of WORCESTER and others. So what you find may be of 'New Hall' type rather than the product of this particular factory at Shelton.

But not a whit the worse for that; and look out especially for the factory's pleasant LUSTRE WARE, pink and silver, and also some delightful, and very modern-looking, bird painting.

Figure netsuke

Netsuke and Inro

These small carvings in ivory have now priced themselves out of the junk shop, but they fascinate many
people who wonder what they are. Unimportant
pieces are not all that dear.

They were used as a toggle on a silken cord, which
the robed Japanese threaded through their wide
sashes to hold their tobacco box, writing set, inro (or
medicine chest) and other objects which you and I
might keep in our pockets or handbags. Every kind of
figure and animal, natural or fantastic, was carved,
and some are quite delightful.

Ormolu

Twenty years ago a dealer had to work really hard to
get a decent price for an ormolu clock, or indeed any
sort of furniture so decorated. Nowadays they are
looking for it, and it doesn't stay in the shops very
long. This isn't very surprising, really, for contemporary painters and sculptors have made us appre-
ciate interesting textures – and ormolu certainly has
that. It also has the ability to acquire a deep and rich
patina. *Real* ormolu, that is, and here we ought, perhaps, to try to get down to brass tacks in more senses
than one.

For it should be noted that what we in this country
call 'ormolu' is quite a different affair from the
French '*or moulu*', that is to say, gold ground down
to a fine powder and used in a mercury amalgam for
gilding. In fact the French word describes the gilding
on the article; whereas the anglicized version of it
refers to the piece itself, usually brass covered with a
lacquer gilding. But there *was* good English ormolu,
even if it never quite had the finish of the French.

Today you can find odd lamp brackets, waiting for

Ormolu clock

the interior decorator to snap them up, or furniture fittings such as drawer handles, table feet and castors, curtain fittings, bas-reliefs.

If you want real ormolu, of course, you must learn to find your way through the maze of Victorian lacquered and electroplated brass alloys. How? The usual way, I'm afraid: either by buying your experience or by taking a first-class dealer into your confidence.

Paintings and Prints
Here is an enormous subject, full of pitfalls for the unwary. Everyone covets an old oil painting, and every owner of one either believes or hopes that it is by a master and, if the truth be known, worth thousands of pounds. Except one man I know, who goes on the principle that every picture offered him which bears a name label or a signature is an obvious fake; and he invites people in to see 'my fake Crome' or 'my bogus Baxter print'. But I suspect that even he hopes that one day he will turn out to have been mistaken.

For the truth is that clever people can do pretty well anything to make an oil painting look like an undetected masterpiece of fabulous worth, by methods ranging from covering it with dust and grime, to repainting it with bismuth so that it becomes as cracked as an old teapot. Much of this copying was done generations ago – leaving plenty of time for re-touchings and re-paintings to settle down to a quiet old age.

Subject is the main stock-in-trade of the dealer anxious to get rid of these things. A mill by a river with a boat, and you have Constable; a flower painting, and it's certain to be Walscappelle; anything covered with a good rich brown sauce is, to the really knowledgeable, a Claude; while a lady in a big hat with an ostrich feather is definitely by Gainsborough, or one of his pupils.

You have to remember, of course, to keep a sense of proportion. No self-respecting artist will paint you an oil painting today for less than twenty pounds – the canvas and colour alone can cost him seven pounds. So you can hardly expect to get a good example of, say, the Dutch sixteenth-century school for a couple of quid. Even a water colour of any virtue must be worth a few pounds although as a matter of fact I have seen excellent ones going a lot cheaper than that.

If you want an infallible rule for never getting swindled, may I suggest the following? That in buying a picture, whether it is an oil, a water colour, a print or what have you, go by nothing else but its worth *as* a picture. In other words, you decide that the picture is well composed, the 'values' are right, the paint well-handled, the whole thing done with taste and good judgment: and that, in addition, you like it. Then give whatever you can afford for it and hang it on your wall. If somebody comes along one day and offers you a fortune for it, that's fine: if they don't you've got a picture you like and to the devil with everyone else.

As to prints, it may help to sort out some general categories, so that we know roughly what we are looking at. In particular the inscriptions you see at the bottom of them.

First, you can have an engraving which is an 'original', i.e. the artist started the picture from scratch. Alternatively, it can be engraved 'after' a painting or a sculpture. In this case you will find the original artist referred to by the term 'delin.' or 'del.' which means *delineavit*, or 'drawn by'; while 'sculp.', or 'sc.' will stand for *sculpsit*, or 'engraved by'.

Now for the different sorts of prints. *Line engravings* are cut on a metal plate with a V-shaped tool called a burin, while *aquatints* and *etchings* are bitten out of the metal by successive baths in acid. With *mezzotint*, you work the copper plate over with a steel tool until it is covered with minute points, and then scrape these down to give wonderfully subtle tones which make it ideal for reproducing paintings. In *drypoint* the 'burr' thrown up by the engraving tool is left to give a velvety black. *Woodcuts* were the most popular form of book illustration in the nineteenth century, while *lithographs* depend upon the fact that oil and water are not happy together. A design is drawn with greasy chalk and the stone damped with water; the ink adheres only to the greasy parts.

There are many sorts of prints to be found today. Bookshops are breaking up illustrated books to sell separately small hand-coloured aquatints of uniforms, views, birds and flowers. The famous Redouté roses have been reprinted and can be bought for five shillings upwards. Baxter prints, which used an early four-colour process, are hard to find, and so are those of Bartolozzi, another famous name in the print world. Early Japanese colour prints from wood blocks, which so fascinated the French impressionists, appear at the bigger sales, but modern reprints of Hiroshige and Hokusai are coming in still.

What you have to decide about prints, I feel, is whether you merely want some pleasant pictures about the place, or whether you intend to become a serious collector, keeping your finds in cabinets. In the latter case I would recommend you to start among the fairly small number of shops which specialize in prints and learn there the significance of 'early states', (i.e. impressions taken early in the progress of work on the plate) or of 'signed artists' proofs' and so on. In these shops you will find the work of fine artists like Short, Cameron, Whistler, Muirhead Bone, McBey, to mention the English ones only, at prices from 15*s.* up to £60 or more. Such things are 'originals' in the sense that the engravers or lithographers usually worked on these impressions themselves.

But if it is simply a question of wanting a picture for the wall, caring naught about oils, water colours, prints, etc., there are all those reproductions (it is confusing to call them 'prints') of the world's masterpieces from Leonardo da Vinci to Bernard Buffet which are now to be found in the art shops. Here you can make your choice between letterpress, printed from blocks; photogravure, an etching process which gives greater richness of tone; offset lithography, a modern version of traditional lithography; and a refinement of it called collotype which has such a natural blending of tones as to give probably the most exact reproduction of the original picture.

Papier-mâché letter rack

Papier Mâché
I remember once as a child being absolutely spell-
bound by the sight of a large tray in a shop window.
I suppose it was an antique shop, but in those days I
wouldn't have known. Anyway there was this tray,
which was jet black, and in the centre of it a beautiful
painting of an abbey or a church.

For me it was something right out of the middle of
a novel by Scott, for the windows glowed with a
pinkish light on one side of the tower and a greenish
one on the other. Obviously, one window was reflect-
ing the light of the moon, while the other showed the
glow of a fireplace. Who could be sitting at that fireplace? What was going on behind that window?

Little did I know it but the tray was made of papier
mâché and no doubt it was going begging for a pound
or less.

From the eighteenth century up to mid-Victorian
times, this highly popular material was used for furniture of all types, not only trays but screens, workboxes, writing cases, vases, even chairs, tables and
cabinets. Many of them are beautifully painted in oil
colours, sometimes with views, sometimes with
flowers or designs in CHINOISERIES, like those on the

black Japans that were fascinating European designers at that time. Long after seeing my tray I discovered that my two glowing windows were not actually mother of pearl, as my elders then told me, but nautilus shell, pressed into the oil of the painting before it dried.

Trays seem to have survived in greater numbers than anything else, except perhaps for WORKBOXES: probably this is because of late years they will have been used for ornament rather than carrying things. Most papier-mâché items seen in the junk shops are in need of repair, but it seems that the 'trade' has resources for putting this right.

Parian

Statuesque white ladies, sometimes in flimsy draperies, sometimes with none on at all, but always contriving to cloak themselves with an air of mid-Victorian modesty, are outstanding items in Parian ware.

It emerged in the eighteen-forties as an attempt to re-create the wonderful unglazed BISCUIT porcelain of DERBY. Both COPELAND and MINTON were separately engaged in the search for statuary porcelain, as they at first called it, and they eventually named it after the marble from the Greek island of Paros. Wedgwoods made a version which they called Carrara ware, after the famous marble, while Adams, DAVENPORT, WORCESTER, GOSS and Ridgeway also joined in the fun.

What Parian did was to bring classical or neo-classical style statuary, such as was being made all over Europe at that time, down to a size that would fit into the middle-class drawing room. Famous pieces like Hiram Powers' 'Greek Slave' were best sellers, as were the various versions of Venus. My own specimen

Parian ware

piece of it is Minton's version of 'Dorothea', the
character from *Don Quixote* dressed (only just) as a
shepherd, for which I paid seven pounds. Since then I
have seen one going for only four pounds ten, so either
I paid too much or the price has come down.

Types of Parian in the shops today include, first,
these statues, sometimes bearing the name of the
sculptor, sometimes marked with that of Benjamin
Cheverton, which means that the figure was reduced
from the full size by means of the machine which he
invented; second, there are some quite charming
figures and groups of children; third, a whole variety
of portrait busts, either of classical figures or men and
women of the day, all varying greatly in size, from a
few inches to several feet. There are also wall PLAQUES,
perhaps the most frequently met with being the
famous pair 'Night' and 'Morning' of Thorwaldsen.

Sometimes Parian is tinted – I have seen large figures in a pleasant pale green – while in others the white Parian biscuit porcelain is set off by a glazed background.

There is a good deal of picking over to be done in this field. If a great deal of Parian is apt to be mawkish and sentimental, there is some which is very good; and with the best of it one always has to admire the quality of the material and the excellent craftsmanship of the modellers.

Patch Boxes

I have never seen a patch box in a junk shop which I thought worth buying, and in any case, such little boxes were made by the thousand long after ladies gave up the habit of hiding their blemishes under patches. But see 'BATTERSEA'.

Pâte-Sur-Pâte

Literally 'paste-upon-paste'. It refers to a technique of decoration introduced into Mintons about 1870 by Marc Louis Solon.

It was an incredibly painstaking process whereby a relief design is applied not by sticking on a relief in the way of JASPER WARE, but by actually modelling it with brush strokes, using a transparent slip, or very thin batter of paste. These designs, usually classical in style, were done on a dark blue background, which showed through and so provided the tones, or shading.

Solon generally signed his pieces Miles or M.L.S., and they are – as they always were – very expensive.

Pembroke Table

A smallish table with a comparatively long top and

short flaps, supported by brackets. Appears to have
originated about 1760. Nearly opposite in design to a
SUTHERLAND TABLE.

Pewter

This famous and popular alloy of tin and other metals
is one of those fields which you can pass by for years –
and then suddenly get interested and become a
fanatic.

It isn't, I believe, bought so much by the general
public as, say, thirty years ago, probably because of
the decline of oak, which it goes with magnificently –
having, so to speak, grown up with it. But to judge by
the prices asked by specialist dealers, there is certainly
no lack of collectors to pay high prices for interesting
pieces from the eighteenth century and earlier.

So far as our junk shop quest is concerned, except
by strokes of real luck, we will have to limit ourselves
to early Victorian wares, such as the measures and
drinking pots, the inkwells and mustards and peppers,
spoons, feeding cups and chimney ornaments, small
toys, tobacco stoppers, SNUFF BOXES and the rest.

If you are going to look out for measures, you have
a whole range of shapes to sort out, from the early

Silver-style pewter christening cup

'Capstan' inkwell

balusters to the straight-sided Victorian ones. In collecting these you can learn a good deal about excise matters, for they were constantly being tested and stamped. I have a half-pint pot which bears marks from 1840 right through to 1857 – did it go into honourable retirement after that?

Some collectors like the tankards bearing the names of inns. Quite recently I picked up for three pounds a parcel of pewter items which included one of the capstan-type inkwells, two great quart pots bearing the names of pubs at Sheerness and Deptford, another attractive but unidentifiable mug with a silver-style handle, a pint pot from the 'Bricklayers Arms, Fairfield Road' (where?), also a small pot marked 'James Dixon and Sons, E.P.B.M.'

This last carries a warning. Anything marked 'Dixon' and most items marked 'Sheffield' with a number, are not pewter, but Britannia metal, a substitute which had no lead in it and tended to follow the styles of silver and SHEFFIELD PLATE rather than of pewter itself. Later in its history this metal was even plated – hence 'E.P.B.M.' stands for electro-plated Britannia metal.

A word about the appearance of pewter. Some people like it in the dull grey colour it falls into without cleaning, and feel that to put a bright polish on it is to make it ape silver. But in fact the colour and appearance of cleaned pewter is nothing like that of silver: it is far more mellow and subtle, especially when seen in firelight. So my view is, give your pewter a good clean when you get it, then keep it up by a good washing and rubbing every few months. Some recommend using a very soft abrasive powder (i.e. one that doesn't scratch) and plenty of elbow grease, so as to keep the fine patina which old pewter picks up in the same way as old furniture. Of course, if a piece is badly oxidized, only acid will serve, but if I were sufficiently fond of a piece to want to get it up into good condition I would prefer to hand the work over to an expert.

Pewter made in recent times contains much less lead – it is limited by law to not more than 10 per cent, which gives it a totally different look and feel from some of the older alloys, with anything up to 40 per cent of lead. Put two specimens together and you will have no trouble in distinguishing them.

If you should come across some really old pewter and wish to identify pewterers' touch marks, then I would refer you to the READING LIST.

Pint measure

Piecrust ware

Piecrust Ware

No doubt you'll have seen in antique shop windows an object which looks like a pastry pie, made of buff pottery.

This is the famous piecrust ware and there is a story to it. During the Napoleonic wars, when our trade with overseas countries was very much restricted by the European blockade, flour became exceedingly scarce, so that the meat and game pies so much favoured in those times had to be served without their crusts. So enterprising potters like WEDGWOOD and TURNER, producers of buff-coloured caneware, made from it dishes which looked exactly like pies, even to the markings on the pastry. People could then cook their hares, rabbits and other game in them *en casserole* and still seem to have one of their beloved pies.

There are still quite a few of these items about, usually priced at about five pounds.

Pinchbeck

How appropriately named is this 'poor man's gold', invented by Christopher Pinchbeck (1670–1732), a London maker of watches and other items.

A warm gold colour, it does not usually tarnish, and is often found on small boxes, on Georgian and early

Victorian jewellery, little boxes and lockets. It was an alloy of copper and zinc, and it was gradually superseded by low-carat gold. But it has a charm of its own, and is well worth hunting for.

Pincushions

There was a day when we were all held together by pins, and that also was the day of the decorative pincushion. These are still about, often with their tender messages for happy expectant mothers: 'Bless the Babe and spare the Mother' – a grim reminder this, perhaps, of days when motherhood was a major risk. The same thought is expressed in

> *Welcome little innocent*
> *Welcome to the light of day*
> *Smile upon thy happy mother*
> *Smile and chase her fears away.*

They also came in different shapes, sometimes as hearts (from sailor friends and admirers), sometimes diamonds, while much more ambitious were those in the shapes of little coaches, spinets, bellows, etc., made up with two solid sides of wood, or of mother of pearl and IVORY, etc.

Gilt pincushion

Sunderland lustre plaque

Plaques

There's an inexhaustible quest here. For wall decoration, plaques have a much longer history than pictures, and when they are made in metals they have a much longer life – though many will have succumbed to that inevitable hazard of metal, the melting pot. But they also come in IVORY, ENAMELS, bone, EARTHENWARE and PORCELAIN.

Without trying to be too exhaustively historical, let's look at a very assorted few I have possessed in the last few years.

Item: There's a brass cut-out plaque made for the Victorian cottager's mantelpiece. It shows a family round a table horrified at having killed the goose that laid the golden eggs. The brass is a bit scratched and worn, but that only makes it look authentic. One comes across cast-iron plaques of this sort, and on some of them you can still see the traces of bright colours. If you dated these in the first half of Victoria's reign you wouldn't be far out.

Item: There's one of the famous 'Sunderland' plaques in printed earthenware, with LUSTRE borders, bidding me prepare to meet my God. I'd like to change this one day for one of those more cheerful ones showing a sailor's return, or perhaps the 'Farmer Arms'. Views of the Wearmouth Bridge are much seen, and of course the border is generally in that 'bubbled' version of pink LUSTRE achieved by blowing oil through a tube.

Item: There's a JASPER WARE plaque by Wedgwood showing a classical frieze. These are sometimes mounted in panels, or framed, or even set in plaster.

Item: There's a largish oval enamel plaque painted in pink with an eighteenth-century lady's portrait. I've no idea where this came from, but it only cost ten shillings and I suspect it's French.

Item: There are various BONE CHINA ones painted with flowers and more likely intended for pot and plant stands than to hang on a wall. Perhaps these should be classified as TILES.

Item: There is a French porcelain one (no idea which factory) framed in ORMOLU, with a landscape.

Parian plaque

Item: There's a small bronze one which I bought because the finely worked relief of the Judgment of Solomon had a look of Breughel about it. I didn't suppose it had been done by Breughel, for so far as I know the great Dutchman never carved a relief in his life; but without prompting on my part the dealer suggested early eighteenth century Dutch, and as I liked it anyway it didn't seem dear at a pound. Probably from the plinth of a vase or cabinet.

Item: There are a pair of PARIAN plaques (already mentioned under that head) by Thorwaldsen, called 'Night' and 'Morning' and showing an angel bearing children in her arms, in one case to their slumbers in the other to the excitements of a new day. I have seen these in terra cotta and they are based on originals which are, or were, at Chatsworth.

Plaques, I suspect, are undervalued at the moment for reasons of fashion.

Pole-Screen
A kind of FIRE SCREEN.

Pontypool and Usk Ware
'Round as a Pontypool waiter', is an old catch phrase, and it refers, not to a portly man in an apron, but to a small circular tray made of japanned tinware.

Few things keep their period charm like the teapots, tea-trays, coffee pots and urns, kettle braziers and other items in this ware, which would stand up to heat, wear and tear, and yet carry some of the most attractive decoration you could wish for. The grounds of green, sapphire, puce and orange are especially admired.

The story of the trade carried on in the Welsh towns of Pontypool and Usk by the Allgood family in

M

the late eighteenth century is a fascinating one. But
most of the examples of this sort of ware one sees
nowadays must have been made in the mid-nine-
teenth century, when the Welsh industry had died
away to a trickle and the business had been taken up
by Birmingham and Wolverhampton.

Porcelain (Hard Paste)

Here is the aristocrat of the world of ceramics. Over
twelve hundred years ago the Chinese discovered how
to fuse together two forms of a felspathic rock at a very
high temperature and so produce a material of great
beauty such as has never been seen before.

Porcelain can be terrifyingly thin. (There is a kind
called – with very good reason – 'eggshell' porcelain.)
It can also be massively thick and strong. (You can
buy a barrel-shaped garden seat made of it, and if
you sit an eighteen stone man upon it, he may hide
the decoration but he will not break the seat.)

When porcelain is thin it is translucent, that is to
say you can see light through it; but this is not the only
test of it, and in fact the Chinese themselves judge
porcelain far more by the resonance of its ring. They
also go by its 'feel': there is a piece in existence bearing the inscription 'For the Imperial fondling of
Ch'ien Lung'. But perhaps the chief means of identification is the fact that as glaze and body are fused
together as one, a broken piece will show a clean glassy
fracture, not a chalky or sugary one as with other
sorts of ceramics.

CHINESE PORCELAIN (and also European after its re-
discovery in the eighteenth century) is known as true
or HARD PASTE porcelain. But before that re-discovery
– and even after it in England – a substitute for it was
produced called:

Porcelain (Soft Paste)

and this is what we now treasure as the product of eighteenth-century CHELSEA, BOW, LOWESTOFT, BRISTOL (LOWDINS), CAUGHLEY, Pinxton, Nantgarw, SWANSEA, early WORCESTER, DERBY, and some European factories.

Made by mixing clay, lime, soapstone and other items with ground-up glass it looks almost 'home-made' compared with the formidable hard paste from the Continent, but the imperfections and irregularities are part of its charm. Its glaze shimmers unevenly; it seems to have been put on as an afterthought while the potter was looking out of the window at the daffodils. It breaks with a sugary fracture, and it can be filed with a nail-file – if you can bear to think of doing such a thing!

Surprisingly enough you can still buy modest pieces of it in junk shops. In a disreputable-looking old furniture store, in a provincial back street, I bought for 10s. a nice CAUGHLEY 'BLUE AND WHITE' scalloped edge plate with the 'Fisherman' pattern. It was proudly displayed on a dresser along with several pieces of STAFFORDSHIRE PRINTED EARTHENWARE plate.

You can find cups and saucers for a pound or two, and five pounds will buy a pretty cream jug or a dish. This may sound a lot, but nobody will ever make this ware again, and it has something which no later things have ever achieved. So get yourself some 'soft paste' before it is too late – and before you remember that you can't afford it!

Posy-Holders

Has it ever occurred to you, madam, to carry a posy when you go to a party?

It would have been very correct a hundred years

Posy-holder

ago and you would have equipped yourself with a posy-holder either of mother-of-pearl, of gilt-metal pressed and fretted to look like expensive filigree work, or – if you were a real swell – of gold, silver, or porcelain.

In the early Victorian days they actually carried these attractive little things in the hand, and some of them have a tripod, so that you can stand them down if and when a gentleman asks you to dance.

There are a number of shapes and all sorts of materials but you will have to look a little hard for them nowadays, especially those delightful affairs made of interlaced leaves and flowers.

Potlids
You will undoubtedly have seen at some time or another small round lids printed with colour pictures. They are what is known as pot-lids, and are the quarry of an increasing number of collectors.

When genuine (and not specimens printed hopefully by modern potters using the old plates and a little skill in ageing) they are an early form of selling goods by packaging design. They were the lids of pots carrying such necessities as bear grease – a dressing for gentlemen's flowing locks of early Victorian days – also fish paste, meat paste, and many other products. Today you can sometimes see them in a dark wooden circular frame, which is how many people like to keep them, hanging a group of them on the wall.

Except for the rarer specimens – which usually means the early ones – potlids do not normally cost more than two or three pounds. But good ones take some finding, and serious collectors find it pays to go to specialist shops rather than hunt through the dull and wretched ones usually seen in the general junk shop. The better ones are often quite charming, and bring to life most vividly the Victorian scene, its heroes and

Potlid

heroines, its everyday occupations, its sports and pastimes.

Most of the early ones were made by F. and R. Pratt & Co., of Fenton, Staffs, whose senior partner, Jesse Austin, developed especially for these lids a multi-colour printing process similar in many respects to the method used for Baxter prints. For his subjects he copied pictures by famous artists of his own and earlier days – Gainsborough, Landseer, Mulready, Wilkie, Webster, and so on; but some were originals, by Jesse himself.

The rarest and most keenly sought after are the early 'bear' motifs (for the bear-grease pots); these usually showed bears at play or in action against hunters. Then there are views of the Great Exhibition of 1851, panoramas in London and other large cities, country landscapes and scenes, portraits of celebrities and literary characters, sports and games, also *genre* pictures showing people going about their lawful (and sometimes unlawful) occasions.

Colour printed plate

As already mentioned, the forger is in the land here as elsewhere, using the original copper plates for his coloured printing transfers, and producing something so much like the original lid that many buyers are taken in. In Mr H. G. Clarke's book mentioned in the READING LIST, a good many of the designs with 'modern editions' are listed so as to forewarn the collector. False ones usually stand accused by their unconvincing colours, a lack of 'crazing', and a different sort of 'ring'. When struck gently with another plate the genuine one in most cases will sound dead, while the false one will ring.

Other firms besides Pratt made these potlids, and, conversely, the pictures themselves were used on a wide range of plates and other 'useful' wares, sometimes with a relief decoration round a deep rim. These are often called PRATTWARE in the trade, a term which is already in use for those early figures, jugs and other wares made by this same firm of Pratt (and others too of course) in an earlier generation. While on the subject of potlids, don't overlook the possibilities of the pots themselves, such as this race of mustard pots in

Mustard pot

blue or white glazed earthenware with bronze
transfer printing.

Pottery

This word can mean anything made by a potter, or it
can be used to denote EARTHENWARE or STONEWARE,
as distinct from PORCELAIN or CHINA. As, therefore,
the term isn't much use as a means of identifying
anything, I suggest that you start looking under these
other heads and go on from there.

Prattware

You may sometimes have seen in the better class of
shop a type of EARTHENWARE in a very distinctive
sort of orange, blue, green and yellow. If they were
not so naïvely and unmistakably English you might
think they were foreign imports – say Italian. Sometimes you will see a jug, or one of those five-holed
FLOWER HOLDERS, more rarely a simple PLAQUE,
showing perhaps a milkmaid with a cow.

This class of pottery, chiefly associated with Felix
Pratt of Fenton, Staffs (1780–1859), but made in

Prattware jug

many other places as well, emerged somewhere about
the end of the eighteenth century and continued for
about thirty years. The relief jugs, often bearing
portraits of Nelson and Admiral Vernon, make high
prices now, while the unique and charmingly absurd
little figures are real collectors' pieces.

The term PRATTWARE is also applied to later
Staffordshire wares which have been printed with the
same coloured pictures as appear on POTLIDS. This is
understandable enough since a later generation of the
same family was engaged in making them.

'Miser' purse

Purses

Purses and little money bags are sometimes seen about,
especially those made of beads or net, most of them
made at home by the busy fingers of wives and
daughters. Some were in silk, some a network of gold
and silver thread, and there were many in jet.

The 'miser' purse is a curiosity of Victorian days.
They are long purses with an open fold in the middle
for the coins, which were kept in place by sliding
along rings of metal.

Puzzle Jugs

One of the many items in JOKE POTTERY AND GLASS,
which see.

Rockingham

Who has not seen some delightful Rockingham cups
and saucers in an aunt's corner cupboard and longed
to have them?

Puzzle jug

Pottery was first made at Swinton, near Rotherham, on the estate of the Marquis of Rockingham, in the middle of the eighteenth century. Its teapots and other wares decorated with the brown 'Rockingham' glaze became famous and have given the name to a glaze used on pieces made everywhere down to the present day.

But ROCKINGHAM bone-china seems to have begun when a family of potters named Brameld moved in and made a ware noted for its richness and extravagance of ornament, even in a day when most potters went to town in this way. King William IV paid £5,000 – a huge sum in those days – for a dinner service, and the nobility vied with each other to buy similar wares. But the ambitiousness of the Bramelds got them into financial trouble and although helped by the Earl Fitzwilliam, they finally gave up in 1843.

There is still plenty of Rockingham china in the shops, chiefly the tea-services we began by talking about, with buff, pale blue or grey grounds and lace-work gilding. The most usual mark is a Fitzwilliam griffin, but pieces also bear the name of Brameld or Rockingham. The addition of 'Royal' signifies a

Rockingham teapot

date later than 1830, when King 'Billy's' set was made.

Rolling Pins (Glass)

Rolling pins of glass are still plentiful enough in the shops.

They fall into several groups. First, there are the solid dark ones, made of bottle glass and flecked with coloured enamel glass: these are referred to under NAILSEA, and are usually attributed to that place, although they are just as likely to have been made at Stourbridge, Wrockwardine or any other glassmaking centre.

Then there are the hollow ones, with a stopper hole at one end. Some of these are in the Nailsea-type bottle glass, but others are in clear glass, often bearing a picture of a ship, or a motto, or a loving message from a sailor to one or other of his sweethearts.

It has been variously suggested that these items were designed (a) to hold, and keep free from damp, the household salt and sugar – then very costly; (b) as love tokens; (c) as chimney corner charms against spooks; and (d) just as rolling pins. My theory is that they were probably used at one time or another for all these things. The hollow ones with messages

Glass rolling pin

could have been bought by our ever-constant sailor filled with tea or sugar or sweets, and when empty used as a container. If they were used for salt, the best place to hang them was over the chimney, for this would not only keep the salt dry but, according to the wise ones, infallibly discourage any evil spirits that lurked in the house.

Or they could have been used quite simply as rolling pins, filled with cold water. Every good pastrycook knows that both cool hands and a cool roller produce the best results; and as a matter of fact you can today buy highly efficient modern versions of these glass water-containing rollers in your hardware shop.

You can also, I'm afraid, buy highly efficient reproductions of the ones discussed above, with just sufficient age and signs of wear on them now to look old.

Salopian
Name and mark used on the wares made at CAUGHLEY.

Satin Glass
This is the name given to a type of glass with satiny shaded tones of red, yellow and blue. You often see rose-bowls or cream jugs made of it, and some of the more ambitious pieces are making a bit of money now. Especially the lamps, in the light of which this particular type of glass glows entrancingly.

Sealed Bottles

Sometimes you will come across an old bottle, of a
dumpy or otherwise irregular shape, with a small
piece of glass stuck on the shoulder like a seal. On the
seal there are some letters or a design.

These are old English 'sealed' wine bottles and
they make excellent quarry for anyone interested in
local or national history. For 'sealed' doesn't mean
'stoppered' or closed up but simply refers to the seal
or label of glass, bearing the insignia of its owner.
The seal was stuck on at the time of manufacture and
quite often bears a date.

These bottles go back to at least the 1650's, when
they began to supersede the charming DELFTWARE
wine bottles we have discussed under that head. The
early glass ones mostly belong to the great houses or
university colleges, where the wine was purchased in
casks and the bottles used for sending it to table.
Later on, this custom spread to inns, and later still
vintners began supplying them to ordinary houses,

Sealed bottles

sometimes with their own marks upon them, sometimes with the customers' initials.

Shapes of these bottles have changed down the ages, following changes in customs. For example, in the early days they roughly followed the styles of their DELFTWARE and STONEWARE predecessors in being short and round-bellied – 'dumpies' they were called. Later on, however, when people began to lay down their wines for keeping, they evolved the cylindrical shape we know today. With the help of the dates on many of the seals, it is thus possible to trace the evolution of bottle shapes down the centuries and also to place undated bottles by their shapes and possibly tie them down to a particular person.

In the book mentioned in the READING LIST, no fewer than 800 seals are listed and their owners include one king, two bishops and about thirty peers of the realm, as well as colleges and institutes.

Sometimes a bottle found in a building or a garden will provide an important clue to a former owner or occupier of a house.

In the end, of course, these sealed bottles were replaced by the flint-glass decanter or the bottle with the printed label, so you don't find them dated much after 1850.

Scent Bottles

There is a lifetime of collecting here, and your way will take you through every department of ceramics, metals and glass and a lot more materials as well.

I would say that you have two main fields in front of you: the rare things of the eighteenth century, in GLASS, ENAMEL, SILVER and gold; or, you go for the more modest nineteenth-century affairs, sold at fairs as lovers' keepsakes.

'NAILSEA' made them, and there are double-ended ones, with one compartment for perfume and the other for some aromatic vinegar used by Victorian ladies when confronted with emotional crises. Odd cut-glass ones from toilet sets are worth looking for, especially if you can date them from the SILVER mounts.

And what of the similar *bijouterie* of the future? Don't laugh, but has it occurred to you that one day someone will be collecting those little glass bottles on your dressing-table, long after they have shed the paper labels of famous perfumiers? Some of them are most beautifully designed and made, even if they *are* factory products; in fact, they could be the CHELSEA and BATTERSEA of tomorrow. So if you want to be remembered by your great-grandchildren as a very wise old bird (or girl, as the case may be) fill a box with them and stow it away in the attic.

Semi-China, Semi-Porcelain
Names for the tough sort of table earthenwares known also as, and described under, STONE CHINA.

Sèvres
As well as a factory for the manufacture of PORCELAIN, both HARD PASTE and SOFT PASTE, this is a symbol of luxury in ceramics, perpetuated in this country by the many imitations of it made during the nineteenth century by COALPORT, MINTONS and many others.

Started about 1745 and taken over by Louis XV in 1752, the factory's early productions include the famous BISCUIT porcelain, with its delightful figures by Falconet and others, the decorated wares with coloured grounds like *bleu de roi*, *bleu turquoise*, and the

famous *rose Pompadour* (*not rose du Barry*, as we call it
in England, for Louis' second lady friend didn't arrive
at court until much later).

There was also much beautiful painting, both from
Sèvres and from the English factories which imitated
it. There is a legend that a famous piece of Sèvres,
long accepted as a perfect specimen of the French
factory, was sent to one of our own nineteenth-
century establishments for copying: the owner had
to be informed that, despite the 'crossed L's' mark, it
was a piece of their own manufacture.

Sèvres went on producing wares down to the last
century, but this, like all pieces bearing the genuine
crossed L's, has long since passed out of the junk
shops.

Sheffield Plate

The first time I took any real note of Sheffield Plate
was when I saw on the top shelf of a junk shop a pile
of candle snuffer trays. Blowing off the dust I found
they all had a coppery colour showing through the
silver. I asked the man about them and he said: 'Old
Sheffield Plate, guv. They're waiting to go off for

Sheffield Plate snuffer tray

re-plating.' After they'd got their new coating of electro-plating, it seemed, they'd eventually find their way into some more attractive shop. They might even be helped along by having a little of the electro-plating scraped off to let the customer see by the copper that they really were old Sheffield plate. For, of course, the worn piece, displaying its genuineness to the world, is much preferable to one which has been re-plated.

But Sheffield plating isn't the same as electro-plating, and in fact, it owes its demise about 1850 to the invention of that process. It has been called the poor man's silver (a title one might question on seeing the prices fetched nowadays by good pieces!), and appeared somewhere about 1750 when, the story goes, a man called Boulsover happened to be heating a piece of copper in a vice. On stuffing a sixpence in to keep it firm, he found afterwards that he had fused these two metals.

Whether eighteenth-century metalworkers really were as carefree as all that with the price of a gallon or so of beer may be doubted: but somewhere around that time and in that place an industry grew up based on the fact that you can fuse a thin sheet of silver on to a thick slab of copper, roll it out flat and thin, then work this up into (within limits) the same sort of wares as the silversmiths produce.

And in fact nowadays you are really better off buying your Sheffield plate from the silversmith, or at any rate the metal specialist, than the general man – until you learn to find your way about things like re-plating, also about one or two substitutes. For example, soon after seeing the above-mentioned snuffer tray I happened to inherit one, together with a pair of snuffers, among some family treasures. The

N

tray was Sheffield plate all right, with just enough
silver left on to make it attractive when polished up.
But the pair of snuffers puzzled me. Where *they* had
worn, it showed not copper as you would have expected, but iron, or more probably steel. How on
earth could this be Sheffield plate?

The answer was that it wasn't: it was close-plating
– something which seems, in fact, to be more valuable.
I found this out because on the knife blade there was
a maker's mark and name, and the firm was a maker
of close-plated ware. This was quite a different process
from Sheffield plating. Instead of fusing the silver on
to copper before working up the sheet, you made up
the desired piece in some base metal, then applied a
thin layer of silver afterwards, using tin as a solder.
This process pre-dated Sheffield plating, but it was
revived for a few years in the early nineteenth century, and specimens are sought after.

Then there is the trap of Britannia metal. I fell
right into this one, and didn't come out quite so well
as with the snuffers. I thought that anything silvery
looking with 'Sheffield' and no silver mark might
reasonably be considered Sheffield plate. So I paid
a pound for a handsome teapot so marked. Mis-

Sheffield plate teapot

takenly, however, for this word – often with a maker's name as well – can indicate Britannia metal, a cheap alloy similar to pewter: you might call it the poor man's Sheffield plate. Most general dealers think it *is* pewter, and sell it as such when it is in its original form. But when it is electro-plated – as it was in later years, you could easily mistake it for Sheffield plate.

There *are* marks on some Sheffield plate, and they can be studied (see READING LIST). But if you wish to form a serious collection – and it could be an excellent investment – you should look very closely into matters of workmanship, styles, techniques. As always, of course. But you must be prepared to pay for it – people tell me that just now the Americans are more interested in Sheffield Plate than in silver.

Shellwork

People in eighteenth-century England loved the many exotic things which came from the East. Among these were shells, of all kinds and shapes.

Apart from the large CAMEO SHELLS mentioned elsewhere, smaller ones were used for decoration, while much use was made of pieces of the linings of shells. Fruit knives and forks, pocket knives, paper knives, fansticks, CARD CASES, were decorated with mother-of-pearl (the lining of the pearl mussel shell), and so were trinket boxes, jewel caskets, mirror frames, in short, every sort of thing where the pleasant qualities of shell can be appreciated.

I should have thought that a gathering together of small things of this kind would be most rewarding. One or two pieces on a stall simply look charming and old-fashioned: but a whole lot could be a revelation of bygone craftsmanship.

Sheraton-style chair

Sheraton

Not always very easy to distinguish from HEPPLE-WHITE, the style named after Thomas Sheraton (1751–1806) generally prefers the straight line to the curve.

Sheraton was a drawing master from Stockton-on-Tees who had served his time as a journeyman cabinet-maker, but who, so far as is known, never made or sold any of the things shown in his *Cabinet-Makers' and Upholsterers' Drawing Book*, and in fact died in great poverty. So if anyone offers you something guaranteed to have been made by Sheraton himself, that man's word should thereafter be accepted with some hesitation.

Silhouettes

Before the days of photography you could go to a painter for a portrait or a miniature, but it would cost you quite a tidy sum, even in those days. If you wanted to be more economical you patronized a professional cutter-out of silhouettes, otherwise known as a shadowgrapher, or silhouettist.

These little black-and-white pictures, which you now see framed on walls, are named after a French

Silhouette portrait

politician named Etienne de Silhouette – not, apparently, because he had anything to do with silhouettes, but because he was a cheese-paring sort of minister who wanted to cut down on all expenditure he considered inessential. In his view, it seems, portraits were wild extravagance: much better save the money and go to one of these modern silhouettists.

The first of them appeared about 1750, and their real vogue lasted for about a century. Many of them were done free-hand, while others were made by means of a machine. The sitter was placed behind a light so that the shadow of the profile fell upon a sheet of paper. A tracing was made of this and then reduced by a gadget which one still remembers as a childhood toy; you ran a point over a large tracing and simultaneously drew a smaller version of it with a connected pencil on another sheet.

There were several types of silhouettes. In its simplest form it was cut straight out of black paper, cloth or other material and pasted on to a white card, then framed. Others were painted by hand in various tones of black or grey so as to pick out features or details of clothes. Some of these are surrounded by

Scissor-work group

gold and tinsel. In more expensive types the silhouette was painted on to the inside of a convex
(bulging outward) piece of glass in such a way that the
image cast a shadow upon a white background, and
so made the portrait stand out in relief.

Quite apart from the portraits of individuals there
are the wonderful little family groups, also landscapes
and sporting scenes, cut out freehand by famous
people like Torond and Edouart and a host of lesser-
known artists.

As well as the professionals, there were, of course,
the amateurs, for skill in this art was regarded as
quite an accomplishment. It was even taught in
schools. These hobbyists produced delightful little
things for their scrap books, some of which occasionally
come to light.

By about 1860, however, the professionals had been
put out of business by the early photographers – or
more probably had become photographers themselves.
The scrapbook-fillers no doubt found it easier and
more interesting to cut out the exciting new colour
pictures being published by the magazines.

Silver

It would be out of place to discuss silver seriously in a
book like this. You *do* come across silver in junk shops,
but if it is English silver there is the hall-mark (see
MARKS, p. 251) and if it is foreign, your guess is as good

as the junkman's. There *are* foreign marks, and it may pay you to study them.

Don't forget that the silver has a basic scrap value, so weight and quality of alloy are important considerations, quite apart from any decorative angle.

Slagware

This sounds a dreadful name for a very much sought after and sometimes a very attractive thing – although I suppose as a name it's no worse than COAL-PORT. Other names include vitro-porcelain (not much better!), marble glass, purple slag, or 'end-of-day' ware.

By way of identifying it, it may help if I say that you see vases of it in a very special and penetrating sort of blue, and they don't quite look like CHINA or GLASS, but something in between. It also comes in a marbled form, either purple, turquoise, opal, green or other colours. You see it too, in something which looks like black, but when put up to the light shows deep amethyst.

Slagware, according to Mr Bernard Hughes (see READING LIST) is really a cross between glass and stone,

Blue slag vase

or at any rate crudities in iron ore. The name 'end-of-day' ware gives you the clue. It seems that where glassmakers found themselves near foundries they would buy up the slag which floats upon the top of molten metal, mix it with flint glass and orychite and so produce a tough opaque material which could be coloured and pressed into moulds, for both 'useful' and ornamental wares. It was called 'end-of-day' ware because this slag was taken off at the end of the day.

Americans are crazy after this stuff, for they have an immense collecting field of their own under the general term of MILK GLASS, and much of ours is very closely related to theirs. It is one of the reasons why this ware, which a few years ago was obtainable for shillings, now makes its pounds.

The firm of Sowerby, of Newcastle on Tyne, have the biggest name in the trade, and vitro-porcelain was their trade term, the mark being a peacock's head.

But there were other firms working in the locality as I have discovered by looking up the registry mark on some of my own pieces. One day, I suppose, all these little firms will be as carefully documented as the eighteenth-century porcelain factories.

Apart from the purple and other marbled pieces, also the blue vases and jugs, there are versions in dead white, such as a jug I have in the form of an upended trout, which cost me two pounds recently. This was made by Heppell's of Newcastle. There is also a range of smaller cream-coloured pieces such as sugars, compôtes, jugs, pretty little pinched-in baskets like the porcelain ones, tea canisters, butters and so forth. Most of these can be traced to a maker and a date by a registry mark.

Cream slag basket

A more ambitious class of item in the blue variety includes flat-faced pilgrim bottles impressed with nursery rhyme pictures: I saw one recently priced at £4 10s. and as it disappeared within a week, I take it that that is the market price.

Delightful as many of these things are I have some misgiving about paying too much for them. It seems to me that since they are only moulded from materials which presumably still exist today there is nothing to stop their being made again, indistinguishably from the old, providing the price made it worth while. And the way prices are going they may very well be.

Slipware

Probably no kind of pot in this country has such a long and unbroken tradition as slipware. It was made in mediaeval times: and it is still being made in country potteries and studios today, largely by the same methods as the old.

Briefly, slipware is EARTHENWARE which is covered wholly or partly with a 'slip', or thin batter of clay, usually of a different colour from the body. You can dip the whole piece in it; you can 'trail' a decoration over it from a tube or bag in the same way as you put initials on a birthday cake; you can 'comb' it to give a marbling effect; you can 'inlay' it by cutting out a design then filling in with a different colour, as with Sussex wares.

Famous early STAFFORDSHIRE slipwares include the large decorated brown and yellow dishes bearing the names of Ralph and Thomas Toft and others, who are presumed to have been potters, although one wonders how the customers let them get away with putting their mark in enormous letters on the front of the piece. Some have held that the Tofts and the other *were* the customers, in which case one wonders what they did with all those dishes, and why other people apparently had to go without.

Of course these are all museum pieces now, and so, pretty well, are the little MONEY BOXES, cream-piggins, jugs, mugs and other things for everyday use, work of a hundred little country potteries down to quite recent times. Still, I've found Victorian cream-piggins in junk shops for a few shillings, also big watering pots with a lovely thick greeny-browny glaze.

All these things have the unique charm of things made sincerely for use by men with an inborn sense of materials and form, and also a feeling of having been cherished for generations – although you will be hard put to it to trace many of them to their homes.

Souvenir China

In the eighteenth century, when you went on a visit, you brought back with you a piece of porcelain marked 'A trifle from Lowestoft' or perhaps a piece of BATTERSEA ENAMEL with some more personal message on it.

In the nineteenth century people went to many more places than Lowestoft, and, of course, in enormously increased numbers. The legacy of this is a huge quantity of souvenir china and glass of every sort and

I have also, up to the time of writing, seven mugs all printed with views in an English town or village – scenes which have now changed out of all recognition – and each mug is subtly different in shape and decoration although clearly of the same family. The differences in shape are probably due to different consignments or different manufacturers.

In a few years' time we will probably be investigating these things and writing learned articles about them. So it seems to me that you could find worse ways of having fun with your shillings than pioneering in this unexplored world of the day before yesterday.

Spode

Here is a name everybody knows, and because of that many a piece of it costs more than a specimen just as good and just as old, but lacking that magic name. Still, the firm founded by Josiah Spode in 1770 deserves this tribute for all it has done over the years – although I expect the Copelands, who now own it, would rather you paid your respects by buying their excellent modern wares!

The original Josiah played a leading part in the development of STAFFORDSHIRE PRINTED EARTHENWARE, and pioneered the production of BONE CHINA and STONE CHINA; he also made JASPER WARE and BASALTES. 'Copeland, late Spode', so often found on the wares, tells the story of how in 1833 William Copeland bought up the business, calling the firm Copeland and Garrett. See also PARIAN.

I have a few pieces of Spode earthenware, but until recently I thought that I would never come across a really early example of the famous early 'BLUE AND WHITE'. Then I came across three plates of one of the 'Caramanian' patterns for ten shillings the lot; so faith in one's luck was restored. The famous 'BLUE ITALIAN' is still being made, and some of the rarer patterns can be worth several pounds apiece.

Spoon Trays

If by any chance you should come across a little china tray shaped like the one on the drawing, don't write it off as just a dressing-table adjunct, or a crazy sort of saucer. It may very well be a spoon tray.

In days when people drank tea out of little bowls, they usually poured the tea into the specially deep saucer and drank out of that (see CUP PLATES). This meant that you couldn't very well keep your spoon in the saucer, so when you'd used it you laid it delicately in just such a tray as this.

They were made by all the important factories, especially WORCESTER, quite early in their history, so they find themselves wherever such wares usually end up, i.e. in the expensive shops. But you just might find one somewhere in that old pile of crockery I keep telling you to search untiringly!

Worcester spoon tray

Staffordshire spaniels

Staffordshire Figure Ornaments

No antique shop is complete without its quota of figures, priced at anything between thirty shillings and fifty pounds, sometimes more.

But those you see there nowadays in most of them are a late flowering: they come from the mantelpieces of the nineteenth century, and they owe very little to those predecessors of theirs which are mentioned under such headings as CHINA FIGURES or salt-glazed STONEWARE.

They were, in fact, the ornament of the people, made in tiny back-street workshops in the Potteries, often by husband and wife working together, or by children on piecework rates, we are told, of about a penny for ten dozen.

It is easy to see why these colourful items were popular in their own day, whether they were the earlier figures for sideboard or cabinet made 'in the round', or those later ones which had a flat back (they're called 'flatbacks') and stood on mantelpieces.

As to their subjects, almost no popular thing, person

or idea of the day was left out. Everyone will have seen the dogs, in their great variety – the sturdy poodles, the large and rather soppy-looking spaniels with baskets in their mouths, the sleek greyhounds, the sporting dogs like pointers, setters, and foxhounds. Makers like Sampson Smith, James Dudson and William Kent were renowned for their dogs, and from their work you could almost trace the history of dogbreeding over the past century and a half – no doubt somebody has!

Then there are the cows, usually made as milk jugs with little lids on their backs, and sometimes accompanied by a farmer or a milkmaid. There are sheep, with their crinkly coats, sitting beside a tree-stump, the much rarer cats, horses and elephants. Strange that there should not be more horses in an age which depended so much upon that animal: but of course they do appear in equestrian groups like the circus pieces, or mounted characters such as Dick Turpin, Wellington, Napoleon or champion jockeys of the day.

Potters also ranged over the whole of the national life as if they were producing illustrated magazines. They depicted historical events like the death of Nelson and the assassination of Marat; they showed literary characters from Dickens and Shakespeare; they covered religious topics like the Widow of Zarepath, the Sacrifice of Isaac, Elijah fed by the ravens, and the Return from Egypt. By the side of the imposing statesmanlike figures of Gladstone and Pitt stood the effigies of boxers, cricketers, composers, writers, soldiers, sailors, thieves, murderers, parsons and the rest.

Items that went on very late in the century were the small groups depicting some ribald domestic scene

Staffordshire 'flat-back'

such as 'Who will wear the trousers?' or 'Last one into bed'. Then there were the contrasting pair, one showing the 'Ale Bench' with its scene of misery and degradation, the other the 'Teetotal Bench', a picture of domestic bliss all right, but of desperate boredom on the part of the husband.

In this field the collector has to be on his guard against modern 'reissues', that is to say, pieces which are genuine enough in that they were made in Staffordshire and from the original moulds, but arriving from there last month rather than last century. There is no difficulty at all about 'doctoring' these things in order to make them look a little more venerable than they really are.

So once again the counsel is that if you want authentic pieces either go to a dealer of standing and get a written guarantee, or make it your business to get to know about materials and styles of painting, things no faker can ever really manage successfully.

Staffordshire Printed Earthenware

Here is the true junkshop quest. Looking for good
examples of the famous early printed domestic earthenware of potters like Spode, Adams, Ridgeway, Steven-
son and the rest – in spite of the high prices some of
them make – is still very much worth while. For if
you know something about the subject you can still
find bargains and windfalls in the most unexpected
places.

Most of the knowledgeable shops have been cleared
of rarities long since, and when they get hold of any
they know what to charge. But it's surprising how
often interesting plates and dishes turn up in the really
junky places, where the contents of old kitchen cupboards have been cleared and piled up into heaps.
And whereas to many people – including quite a few
dealers – a dinner-plate with a blue pattern on it is no
different from any other at home in the kitchen, to
the person who knows a SPODE 'Indian Sports' plate
when he sees one it is worth several pounds. Some
of the American patterns even fetch three-figure
prices.

But you'll need a lot of patience to find them, also
study of the ware itself. Although it's been thoroughly
and keenly collected for many years now, the patterns
aren't all that well documented.

Earthenware printed under the glaze either in the
more usual blue, or in pink, green, black and other
colours, was a staple crockery of the lower and middle
classes throughout the nineteenth century, and huge
quantities of it were exported all over the world. One
uses the term 'Staffordshire' because most of it did
come from there, but it should be noted that a great
deal was made elsewhere as well.

These dinner and tea services and other 'useful'

Spode blue Italian coffee pot

wares were printed either with 'CHINESE' themes like the famous WILLOW PATTERN, with topographical AMERICAN and English views, with hunting and sporting scenes, romantic or pastoral vistas and a host of other patterns or designs.

In all cases the manufacturing techniques were roughly the same. The design was engraved upon a copper plate, which was inked and an impression of it taken on a piece of tissue paper. Then this was transferred to the piece of pottery to be decorated, exactly as, when a child, you stuck a picture of a butterfly on your wrist. When this design had been covered by a glaze and re-fired, it would remain intact for the life of the piece itself. In fact pieces have been fished up from the bottom of the sea after a couple of generations with the printing still intact.

The reason BLUE AND WHITE predominated over the other colours has already been mentioned under that head, i.e. that cobalt was easier to manage than other pigments in the firing process. But the other colours used were quite attractive – more so to some people.

If a piece has a maker's mark on it, identification is usually an easy matter. But of course, this will give the dealer something to talk about, and naturally he will make the most of it, especially if it is that of a famous potter like SPODE or Ridgeway. Much more fun is there in being able to identify the pieces without a mark; you may get your quarry for shillings rather than pounds.

But identification of unmarked pieces isn't at all easy. All these potters shamefully pirated each other's designs and repeated their own in different periods. The first thing to teach yourself is to be able to tell the difference between new and old pieces. Having decided that a plate is actually earthenware printed under the glaze (see 'CHINA'), and not BONE CHINA, PORCELAIN or anything else, you should compare it with a modern dinner plate from your kitchen dresser. You'll find that usually it's much lighter, and also not nearly so 'efficient'-looking. For example, if you cant the plate up so as to catch the light, the old one will have a sort of shimmery look along the glaze; while if you pass your finger round the rim, or even just look at it carefully, you'll probably find three rough little marks round it. These have been left there by the cockspurs which the old potters used to keep the plates from sticking together when they were in the kiln.

Then there are the designs themselves. Although, as already mentioned, potters lifted each other's patterns with reckless abandon, they generally managed to give their wares their own characteristic touch, either in the drawing, the glaze, or the placing of the pattern, or – most helpful of all – by the border, which many seem to have used as a sort of trade mark. There is a whole field of study in these alone.

One point you have to watch is that you are not buying what you might call 'reprints' of the old wares, especially plates. Several of the older potters have lately taken to re-issuing their old patterns for the export market, and rejects from these consignments often find their way into crockery or hardware shops, or on street markets. Of course, if you've learned to distinguish your materials you won't be deceived for a moment. And in any case most of these pieces bear a modern mark.

So there you are: never leave a pile of dinner plates unexamined: you don't know what you may find there.

Stirrup Cups

When every gentleman rode to hounds several days a week, he needed something to keep out the cold, so a stirrup cup was almost as great a necessity as a shaving mug. As the 'dram' was taken in the saddle, the cup did not have to be stood down anywhere, so it could be any shape you liked.

Usually it was fashioned in the shape of an animal's head, and these items have been collected for a very long time now. A gathering of them would cover a very

China stirrup cups

wide range of materials, many of them in the rarer sorts of pottery, PORCELAIN, EARTHENWARE and BONE CHINA. There were also silver ones from Georgian days, inscribed with the name of the hunt.

Animal-lovers will find plenty to interest them here, for they included foxes and other quarry like hares and deer and even fish; among the dogs were foxhounds, greyhounds, bulldogs, setters, Dalmatians and pugs.

But look out for reproductions!

Stone China

Just about the turn of the eighteenth century there appeared an immensely tough and heavy sort of earthenware, glazed so that it could compete with the new BONE CHINA and also PORCELAIN, and called variously STONE CHINA, Ironstone (e.g. MASON'S IRONSTONE), Semi-china, Semi-porcelain, and so on.

Decorations were crude and colourful, usually following IMARI and Chinese styles and often deliberately imitating the cheaper wares still being imported from the Far East. Huge services still come up at the auctions; being practically indestructible they have outlasted the families who bought them a century or more ago.

In these latter days they have a colour and exuberance which is not to be found in table wares today. Some of the giant pieces made in these wares are mentioned under MASON'S IRONSTONE.

Stoneware

If you go on baking a pot in the kiln to a higher temperature than is needed for EARTHENWARE it

Salt-glazed teapot

becomes STONEWARE, and will hold liquid, be immensely tough, and open up all sorts of new possibilities in the way of decoration. You can, for example, polish it, as if it were stone; you can stain it, as with JASPER; you can cut or scratch decorations in the ware itself, as Hannah Barlow did at DOULTONS; or cut through a coloured glaze to the body beneath, in which case you have s'graffiato work.

To make stoneware even more durable, you can throw common salt into the hot kiln, and the fumes thus given off will settle on the piece and give you salt-glazed STONEWARE. In its earliest manifestation in eighteenth-century Staffordshire (like this camel teapot) it is practically priceless, but see also next paragraph.

Stoneware Spirit Flasks
Few things could be better adapted to their purpose than the spirit flasks in salt-glazed STONEWARE which were to be found in inns and gin shops in Regency and Early Victorian times.

You still see quite a lot of them about, for they suddenly dropped out of use, and being eminently tough many of them have survived to fill the cabinets

Stoneware spirit flasks

of collectors. They are not particularly expensive: except for rarities they can be bought for two or three pounds. Probably this is because they aren't regarded as particularly decorative and so *are* only of interest to collectors.

Like those colourful miniatures one sees on the shelves of modern pubs – one day, no doubt, to be collected in their turn – these buff and brown containers of whisky, brandy, rum and gin were designed to draw attention to themselves. They were made of this iron-hard stoneware, presumably because of the boisterous manners and the stone floors of the taverns of those days. They came in an enormous range of shapes – barrels, books, pigs, potatoes, pistols, clocks, policemen's truncheons (then a newish joke!). Others personified famous figures of the day – kings, queens, politicians and so on; while still others cracked jokes, like 'Mrs Caudle's Bedtime Lectures', from *Punch*.

So far as materials go, there are two main types, those with a light buff and brown salt-glaze, and those

covered with a shiny dark brown 'ROCKINGHAM' glaze.
DOULTONS of Lambeth were important makers, as
were Bournes of Derby.

These flasks met their end quite suddenly about
1845, when the heavy glass tax was repealed, and the
shelves of the inns became filled with labelled glass
bottles which showed their contents. Except for a
brief revival in Edwardian days they have not been
seen since.

Swansea

The fine porcelains made at Swansea and Nantgarw
in the early nineteenth century are wealthy collectors' quarry nowadays, and so, to some extent, is the
best of the equally fine earthenware made at the
Cambrian Pottery under the Dillwyns and the Bev-
ingtons, and at the breakaway Glamorgan Pottery.
Much of it follows STAFFORDSHIRE PRINTED EARTHEN-
WARE styles, but there is a 'Swansea' version of the

Swansea white-ware jug

WILLOW PATTERN, and also much original painting. The fine free 'peasant' styles used on jugs and other table wares are lovely stuff. Swansea made a great many kinds of CHILDREN'S PLATES and COCKLE PLATES.

Sutherland Table

Name given to a type of table with a narrow fixed top and very wide flaps which, when up, are supported on folding out legs, not on brackets. It was obviously designed to provide a big table capable of being put in a small space when it was not wanted in its full size. It appeared somewhere about 1860 and remained popular for perhaps fifty years (opposite to PEMBROKE TABLE).

Tea Caddies, Tea Canisters, Tea Chests, Teapoys

There seems to be some confusion about the exact meaning of these terms, partly, I think, because they have been used in different ways at different times. Let's try and make some distinctions.

When tea first appeared in this country in the seventeenth century, it was kept, it seems, in a *Canister*, the word first being used in this sense about 1711. This receptacle could be either of silver, wood, PAPIER MÂCHÉ, tortoiseshell, IVORY, PORCELAIN, SHEFFIELD PLATE, PEWTER, JAPANNED TINWARE, GLASS, EARTHENWARE, STONEWARE or ENAMEL. These items come up frequently at sales, and, of course, follow the price of the particular materials they were made in.

At first, canisters stood on their own, but as tea came into more general use these containers would themselves be contained in a *Tea-trunk* or *Tea-chest*,

Tea caddy

and locked away for safety, tea being extremely costly in those days. Then, somewhere towards the end of the eighteenth century, this chest, instead of being a container for canisters, acquired the tightly fitting boxes we know today, and was called a *Tea-caddy*. The word comes from the Malayan *kati*, a measure equal to about 1⅓ lb., used in the tea trade.

As for the *Teapoy* this is something different again. Many people believe – as I did for years – that a teapoy is simply a PORCELAIN tea canister – I've certainly seen the word used in that sense. But this is a misleading use of the term; the teapoy proper is a piece of furniture which is a sort of cross between a table and a tea-caddy. The piece of furniture itself seems to have originated in the East, for the name comes from the Hindu for 'three' and the Persian for 'foot': and somewhere along the line this three-footed table got itself translated from 'tinpae' into 'teapoy' –

Teapoy

presumably under the influence of tea, as the *Shorter Oxford Dictionary* so nearly says. Later it became the table on which the tea caddy was kept, and then an actual caddy, mounted upon a three-legged pedestal foot. It is in this form that one sees it today, although very infrequently.

Returning to caddies, here is a whole world for the collector. No doubt that plain ones of standard size are cheap – quite exceptionally, I think, in view of the craftsmanship which has been put into them. On the other hand the small, individual ones, especially those shaped as fruits, pagodas, cottages, etc., though eminently shelfworthy, are very expensive.

Caddies come in all the various woods like mahogany, walnut, satinwood, harewood, maple, rosewood, etc., in PONTYPOOL WARE, TUNBRIDGE WARE, PEWTER and so on. Some have rich carving, some are painted, some inlaid with materials like ebony, IVORY or mother-of-pearl, or mounted with silver.

Every house should, I think, have at least *one* caddy, even if it is only a modest one, simply as a tribute to an age when craftsmen really put their hearts into quite everyday work.

Tea Caddy Spoons

On the shelves of silversmiths you will see small spoons or ladles, usually in some very attractive or interesting pattern.

These were once the inevitable accompaniment of the tea caddy, used to measure tea carefully in days

Tea caddy spoon

when it was one of the dearest things on the shopping list.

These spoons come in a wide range of shapes, scallop shells being probably the most frequently met with, but there are others fashioned like shovels, acorns, vine-leaves, jockey caps, hearts, and fish.

Tiles

Tiles fascinate me almost as much as PLAQUES, probably for the same sort of reasons, namely, that they come in endless variety, that they're done in many kinds of ceramics, and that with them you can cover a very wide range of periods and styles at a not very outrageously high cost.

Delftware tile

Looking round at some I have accumulated almost
casually in the last few years, I find I have three
Dutch DELFTWARE ones, showing biblical scenes like
Tobias and the Angel; two which I feel sure are
BRISTOL delftware, with waterside scenes of ships and
houses; and a pair of Victorian glazed earthenware
ones which are evidently part of a 'Country Scenes'
series; one of them having a youthful fishing party
and the other a shepherd's boy. All these seem to have
cost me between 7s. 6d. and 15s. Then there is a very
handsome one, much larger, in turquoise-blue, which
shows, in a mixture of relief and tone, a charming
picture of two little Victorian girls playing on a drum
and a tambourine. I suspect these are MINTON 'majolica' but it is not easy to identify these things – which, I
think, makes collecting them even more fun. I would
dearly love to find a specimen of BRISTOL's (or somewhere else's) BIANCO SOPRA BIANCO, but I'm afraid
that so far the dealers have always been ahead of
me.

Tiles can be framed, and in fact you often come
across sets of them in threes and sixes. They can also
be laid round a fireplace; and if you have one of those
modern monstrosities of made-up 'surrounds' in a

pinky buff, with one square missing at each end for subtle decoration, I would recommend you to strip the whole thing down and have your local builder put some old tiles round it.

Tinsel Pictures

Difficult to run to earth now anywhere but in the specialist shops, but worth knowing about all the same, are those engaging little pictures decorated with tinsel. They usually depict some famous actor of the early Victorian era in a preposterously heroic attitude, with scenes from the play going on in the background.

These things were originally sold as prints, and you could buy your tinsel decoration – stars, dots, helmets, swords etc. – and do your own brightening up. Only a few years ago they could be found quite cheaply, but lately I have only seen them in the theatrical districts like St Martin's Lane, London.

Don't, however, let that stop you looking through every stack of old pictures you come across in the junk shop: after all, they start on their way to these shops from somewhere like that.

Tobacco Jars and Boxes

You may sometimes come across a battered lead box with relief decoration, perhaps traces of colour, and a little figure on the lid. Inside – if you are lucky – is a flat sheet of lead used for pressing down the tobacco which this article contained.

This is only one of the types of tobacco boxes one sees about. Often the relief decoration shows a landscape or even a battle scene. I recently saw one depicting the battle of Sevastopol. With the earlier ones this decoration was cast as part of the main piece, but later it was applied to a plain box.

Lead tobacco box

You also get these boxes in SILVER, PEWTER, iron, pottery, PORCELAIN and BRASS. One interesting family, evidently an early version of the vending machine, were the brass ones with a ha'penny-in-the-slot arrangement used in coaching inns. On putting in a coin a lock was released and you helped yourself to a 'twist'. But apparently there weren't any means of seeing that you didn't take more than your share, for an inscription on one of them reads:

> *Gentlemen, it's for your pleasure*
> *I wait here from day to day*
> *To supply you (when at leisure)*
> *With the weed, who puff must pay.*
> *For half a penny a pipeful take*
> *And pay regard to what I say*
> *Having that, for credit's sake,*
> *Close the lid, or sixpence pay.*

Another smokers' item well worth looking at now are those small round brass and copper boxes used as pouches. They often have interesting pictures or crests on them, and there is much social and general history in them: many have regimental or club crests.

And while in this field don't let's forget those tobacco tampers or stoppers, used to press down the burning tobacco in the bowl, which are mentioned under BRASS.

Toby Jugs

Real old Toby jugs are now as highly priced as any other early Staffordshire ware, but if you simply want a Toby, there is nothing to stop you buying him brand-new from your local china shop.

His full name is Toby Fillpot, and some say the character was based on a famous toper named Harry Elwes, who is reputed to have put away 2,000 gallons of beer in his lifetime. Others favour Paul Parnell, a Yorkshire farmer and grazier who in *his* lifetime drank nine thousand pounds' worth of Yorkshire stingo.

But these are evidently cases of tying up a well-known personage with something that was already there, for the real Toby seems to have originated in, of all places, Italy. We owe the design of the jug to a

Toby jug

popular engraving published about 1761 to illustrate
a song translated from the Italian by a clergyman
named Francis Fawkes. The reverend gentleman's
rendering was as follows:

Dear Tom, this brown Jug that now foams with mild Ale,
In which I will drink to sweet Nan of the Vale,
Was once Toby Fillpot, a thirsty old Soul,
As e'er drank a Bottle or fathom'd a Bowl.
In boozing about 'twas his praise to excel,
And among Jolly Topers he bore off the Bell.

It chanc'd as in Dog-days he sat at his Ease,
In his Flow'r woven Arbour as gay as you please,
With a Friend and a Pipe, puffing Sorrow away,
And with honest old Stingo was soaking his Clay,
His breath Doors of life on a sudden were shut
And he died full as big as a Dorchester Butt.

His body, when long in the ground it had lain,
And time into Clay had resolv'd it again
A potter found out in its Covert so snug
And with part of fat Toby he form'd this brown Jug
Now sacred to Friendship and Mirth and Mild Ale.
So here's to my lovely sweet Nan of the Vale.

Many Tobies carry inscriptions, most of them jovial
or provocative. 'It is all out, then fill it again' strikes
a typical note, and so does 'Drink your Ale up, cock
your Tail up'; while 'Not for you, Boney' cocks a
snook at Napoleon across the Channel.

Toby himself appears in all sorts of guises – as a
sailor, a parson, a night watchman, planter, fiddler,
as Punch (with his Judy), John Bull, the Woodman,

Silly Billy and the rest. There are also female 'Tobies', like Martha Gunn and the Gin woman.

As to cost, Toby has been made in almost every kind of ware, from the celebrated Ralph Wood's early work in coloured glazes down to modern pottery: so obviously his price will go according to the rarity of the ware he is made in. Sometimes he gets up into the hundreds; for example, a 'Prince Hal' Toby made £220 at Sotheby's last year.

In view of this, our old helpful friends the fakers have been at it, and if you want rare old Tobies they can make them for you without any trouble at all.

Tunbridge Ware

Or Wood Mosaic, as it is sometimes called. The Victorians loved anything that called for enormous pains in the making. You can take an ordinary wooden box and paint or print a picture on it; but in their view it was much more interesting if the picture, instead of being painted, was made up from the tiny *ends* of hundreds, or even thousands, of little sticks of different coloured woods.

That, roughly, is how Tunbridge ware is made. Slips of different coloured woods, each about half the size of a school ruler, were glued together in blocks

Tunbridge ware box

so as to give a pattern or a picture. Then these blocks were sawn across the end to provide veneer sheets, which were mounted on the article to be decorated.

Over 150 English and American woods were used, and it was apparently a point of honour not to use any colouring matter, although staining effects could be obtained by soaking some of the woods in the famous local spring water.

The craft was carried on all through the nineteenth century in and around Tunbridge Wells, in Kent, and you can still buy articles made of it at no very high price. They include workboxes, tea-caddies, trays, candlesticks, even tables.

Turner

A name you may find (and in fact should most strenuously seek) on:

1. A fine race of STONEWARE jugs, with figures in relief and a chocolate-coloured glaze on the neck (once seen never forgotten). They often have silver lids.

2. A JASPER WARE having different tints from, and for my money preferable to, WEDGWOOD's.

3. CREAMWARE, also rivalling WEDGWOOD's.

The name is that of William Turner of Lane End, established 1762. But of course there were many other Turners in pottery, notably Thomas Turner of CAUGHLEY.

Vase-in-Hand

Vases are usually bought individually, but sometimes they fall into a pattern or type which seems to call for putting together and seeing what they look like.

Vase-in-hand

In an antique shop in Sussex recently I saw about a dozen of the sort which consists of a small vase held in a hand, usually a lady's. They are being made again today, of course, but that's no reason why one shouldn't seek out those made in the past.

I have seen it stated that the idea originated at Worcester in the Kerr and Binns era, but I can hardly believe that it came as late as that, especially when you sometimes see specimens in PARIAN. Those in bone china are very attractive indeed, and will probably take some finding in a year or two.

Vinaigrettes

You will have seen in the better sort of shops tiny boxes of SILVER, perhaps no larger than a postage stamp, having a fretted grille inside. These are called vinaigrettes, and their purpose was to revive ladies in days when a timely fainting fit was one of the few remedies they had against an obdurate male world. It was also a help in an age when bad smells could be found without any trouble at all.

The aromatic 'vinegar' was really acetic acid, combined with some essential oil like cinnamon, lavender or mint, and a little sponge soaked in it was kept under the grille. If you are very lucky, you may

Vinaigrette

find one with the sponge still there. As this 'vinegar' was highly corrosive, most silver vinaigrettes have a gold lining, but they were also made in precious and semi-precious stones, or even in glass, or mother-of-pearl. Apart from the boxes, they came in many shapes; as books, purses, shells, acorns, nuts. Silvergilt and PINCHBECK were also used.

Of course you will not expect to find these often exquisitely made little things in heaps of junk. They are usually to be sought in silversmith's shops. But they have been noted in jumble sales, and if you come across one in an inherited jewel box it may well set you off on a collection of them.

Wash Hand Stands
At least, that's what we used to call them in *our* house. Perhaps the proper name for them is basin stands.

Either way, most of them were banished to the attic or the outhouse the moment h. and c. arrived in our bedrooms and bathrooms. But they are now being brought out again and dusted off, for many people are finding a place for them, not in the bedroom, but in the smart, modern lounge, carrying bowls of flowers or plants. I've even seen some fitted up as radio cabinets, with the lower shelf available for the *Radio Times*.

Prices for them are not all that high – it depends on the period and the wood used, for of course they were made in the noblest eighteenth-century materials as well as in Victorian dress. Among the latter, those that have any character – which means, of course, that are capable of looking like something else! – are very keenly sought after, especially the three-legged ones designed to go into a corner and save space. Later on they seem to have got much larger: so presumably the late Victorians washed themselves more thoroughly.

The very humble deal ones (which just shout of their origin in an attic, with a sleepy-eyed servant girl giving herself a lick and a promise before going down to light the fires) are difficult to deal with, and so are those monsters in mahogany and marble, inlaid with tiles. But I *do* like those little metal tripod stands. The Victorians were good with their beloved cast-iron, and when painted white these can look charming outside the door, or on a window balcony.

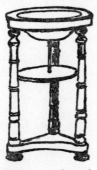

Regency washstand

Wax Fruit and Flowers

Not so very long ago we were rather scornful about
those 'shades' of fruit and flowers made in wax or
other materials which our Victorian grandparents
loved to collect in their crowded rooms. I suppose
they liked them because the more colourful and exotic
fruits and flowers weren't so often to be seen: and
in any case they always admired anything which was
ingeniously made to look like something else.

Nowadays, of course, we are filling up our rooms
again, and these 'shades' are keenly sought after.

Not that they seem to be terribly dear when you
find them. I was offered a pair the other day for thirty
shillings, which, when you come to think of it, can't
be much more than the value of the glass 'shades'
themselves. It's true, there weren't wax fruits inside,
but cloth flowers; but all the same there was a great
deal of work in them, and they looked nice enough.
A third one I saw lately had a bunch of flowers in a
vase-in-hand – in this case in PARIAN.

Very much rarer members of this family are the
shades in which you find paperwork figures; SHELL-
WORK ones are also found.

Flower shade

Queensware coffee pot

Wedgwood

As we've already noted under JASPER WARE, most people tend to overlook the fact that Josiah Wedgwood and his successors made several other important wares besides those lavender-blue articles decorated with white reliefs, which have been so popular since they first appeared nearly two hundred years ago.

In fact, Wedgwood's really outstanding achievement in the view of many people was *Queensware*, his version of CREAMWARE, which in its day led the field, and put DELFTWARE, STONEWARE and, for many purposes, PORCELAIN itself, out of business both here and on the Continent. It was named from services supplied to Queen Charlotte, which earned Wedgwood the title of 'Potter to the Queen'; and production of it has continued ever since. The early examples are beautifully restrained in design, light in weight and very pale in colour.

Before this, Wedgwood had already made wares in the styles of Whieldon, such as cabbage teapots, and pioneered some beautiful work with green glazes, as well as other items in the Staffordshire tradition like agate and tortoiseshell wares. Later he developed

BASALTES; the buff caneware used, for example, in PIECRUST dishes; a dark-red ware called Rosso Antico; and a terra cotta. Afterwards, the firm produced BONE CHINA for a few years at the beginning of the nineteenth century and this may be identified by the name printed under the glaze in red, blue and gold. It was returned to in 1878, and is still an important product at Barlaston, the new home to which the firm moved just before the war from Etruria, the works and village created by Josiah Wedgwood in the eighteenth century.

Most of the other wares have the name in capitals impressed, with initials for the date since 1860 and the word 'England' added since 1891.

There is a good deal of nineteenth-century Wedgwood of various types still to be found, especially the well-known leaf plates in various colours. The prices vary considerably. Some dealers appear to inflate their prices whenever there is a mark, but of course, Wedgwood 'useful' wares of these later periods cannot be thought of as scarce.

Willow Pattern

As with TOBY JUGS, someone must have been printing earthenware with the Willow Pattern on every working day since it first appeared reputedly in the 1780's, at CAUGHLEY, in Shropshire. It isn't an original Chinese design, as most people imagine, but it is said to have been worked up from a number of Chinese motifs by Thomas Turner or one of his assistants at Caughley. Herbert Minton, founder of the great potting firm of that name, also worked on the original plates, and when he left Caughley to become a freelance designer he made a number of different versions of the design which he sold to other

potters. This accounts for all those variations in the
number of figures on the bridge, the number of trees
and the apples on them, the relative position of the
pagoda and so on, which nobody has ever really
sorted out. Hundreds of potters used the design all
through the Victorian era, so the job of doing so
would be a pretty formidable one.

All this rather plays havoc with the famous legend
which seems to have grown up some time after the
design was worked out. This tells how a Chinese
mandarin once had a lovely daughter named Koong
Shi, and had promised her to a wealthy old merchant.
But Koong Shi was in love with Chang, her father's
young secretary, and when the father discovered this
he locked her up in her room overlooking the river.
Chang managed to float a message down to her in a
coconut shell, and they eloped just as the wedding
preparations were going on. The mandarin chased
them, and on the bridge you see him running after
the fugitives. They hid in the small house on the left,
but the furious mandarin burnt it to the ground:
whereupon the sympathetic gods intervened and
changed the lovers into a pair of turtle doves.

Variations on the Willow Pattern are well worth
looking for: in the last year or so I suppose I have
seen half a dozen, and probably would have seen a
lot more if I'd been looking for them. And there
would be a lot of fun in trying to pin down the unmarked ones to all those Victorian potters who
climbed on the Willow Pattern band-wagon.

Windsor Chairs

I suppose we all know a Windsor chair when we see
one: if not, there are drawings of some overleaf.

But the odd thing is that nobody seems to know

Dining chair

why it is so called. There is, of course, the old legend that King George IV, when hunting in Windsor Forest, was caught in a shower of rain, and took refuge in a cottage. A chair with spindles and a bow back was brought to him and he liked it so much that he ordered some to be made for Windsor Castle.

The only trouble with this story is that the Windsor chair was so named in print long before the Farmer King was born. Moreover, so far from being an outcrop of Berkshire, it appeared everywhere from Lancashire to Somerset at about the same sort of era.

What appears to have happened, in fact, is that somewhere in Stuart times there arose a reaction from the heavy oak settles and stools of Elizabeth's reign and people began to buy from their local craftsmen much lighter affairs, made up of sticks and spindles instead of great hunks of wood.

There are endless variations in design, and woods used include beech, ash, willow, yew and elm. But to try to sort all these out into any sort of chronological order would be practically impossible, for the amateur craftsmen in one part of the country went on copying styles long after they had gone out of fashion

'Comb-back', fan back, Gothic, child's, smoker's bow and bow back Windsor chairs

elsewhere. Experts do find some sort of progression but except in the few cases where a maker has left his name or a number on the back of a chair, it's difficult to trace their origin.

There are, however, recognized terms for the different features of the chairs, which enable the various types to be put into categories. Other kinds of chairs are dealt with in *More Looking in Junk Shops*.

Wine and Sauce Labels

Wine labels, or bottle tickets, as they used to be called, still offer a happy hunting-ground for the collector who doesn't mind spending a couple of pounds at a time. They look attractive, they have a family likeness, and they come in a great many different materials. A group of them mounted in a case can look most decorative.

Experts believe that they have their origin in the pieces of parchment which were once gummed to bottles of port and other wines. When the decanter came in, there arose a need for a removable label which would hang round its neck and indicate the contents. As these would be displayed prominently on the sideboard, it was natural to make them in the same styles and qualities as the other things in the dining room, so that in fact, apart from the interest of their names, they provide quite a miniature museum of decorative themes.

Every kind of drink, known or unknown, seems to have had its label, and a collection of them would also be a history of conviviality over the years, with drinks like shrub, sack, arrack, constantia, mountain, Old Tom, Ay Mousseux, and Bucellas sitting alongside the more familiar madeira, hollands, sherry, whisky and port.

Materials include SILVER, ENAMELS, PORCELAIN, SHEFFIELD PLATE, mother-of-pearl, etc., and there is usually a little silver chain for attachment. The shapes are most varied, ranging from crescents, tiger's claws, shells and leaves to simple initials.

As the title of this paragraph indicates, there were, apart from wine labels, others for sauces, essences and perfumes. It is these which attract the lady collector, for they lead her in to fascinating byways. Look at some of these names – from Dr Penzer's books in the Reading List – and try to guess what they are: Bergamot, Frangipanni, Hungary Water, Golden Trasser, Quin Sauce, Soy, Nepaul, Poverade and Milk of Roses.

Worcester

Worcester has about the longest history of any pottery in this country; so long, in fact, that we will have to chop it up into pieces.

First there was the early factory for PORCELAIN (SOFT PASTE), established in 1751 by, among others, the Dr John Wall whose name is given to the products

Dr Wall teapot

down to about 1783. This era, which at first was a continuation of Lowdin's BRISTOL, saw all those delicious wares with grounds in apple-green, yellow and scale-blue, the flower painting, the fantastic birds and CHINOISERIES, and also the printing under the glaze from designs of the celebrated Robert Hancock and others. The mark of the hollow 'C' is well known and imitation Chinese ones were used shamelessly but very inexpertly.

From 1783 to 1840 the Flights and the Barrs owned the business and the marks show their names or their initials in varying order. From the later date the business was taken over by the Chamberlain family, who had broken away from the main firm in 1783 and been manufacturing on their own. 'Chamberlain's Worcester' with variations, and sometimes with the address of the London showrooms, is a frequent mark.

From about 1852 to 1862 the concern was owned by Kerr and Binns, whose initials were used, after which it became the Royal Worcester Porcelian Company, and as such absorbed two other Worcester factories, that of Thomas Grainger in 1889 and that of James Hadley in 1896, whose names also appeared on their wares.

The work of all these periods is, of course, specialist study, but it is usually possible to tie things down by intelligent study of marks and types. Much of the traditional ware is being made again, but it bears the modern mark and cannot be mistaken.

Although the early wares command high prices at sales, it is still possible to gather together a little Dr Wall 'BLUE AND WHITE' for a few pounds, while Victorian Worcester, while not in the same class for many people, has charms which are perhaps more apparent now than was the case a few years ago. For example, there are some attractive jugs, teapots etc. in the form of leaves; while people are also buying those buff and cream ivory wares of late Victorian days, for one sees vases priced at as much as thirty shillings a piece.

Personally, I think the finest way of having a look at Worcester productions as a whole is to go to Worcester itself. There you can be conducted round the factory and see both new and traditional wares made and decorated. You can also visit the admirable and beautifully arranged Perrins Museum.

Pedestal work table

Workboxes

Few things bring back one's childhood so vividly as the rosewood workbox, perhaps inlaid with IVORY or mother-of-pearl, with a silk-lined tray inside the lid. You see these about, of course, but usually needing repair, for these were for use rather than ornament. PAPIER MÂCHÉ ones are very often seen and even these can be repaired. Sometimes the workbox shades off into a 'pouch' table with legs, or even into a full-blown compendium, with room for games as well.

If you are lucky you will find inside them some of the fascinating things described under NEEDLE AND THREAD.

Fitted workbox

Reading List

General

Since the war a whole library of books have appeared on antiques in the accepted sense of the term (see Introduction).

Some of these are mentioned below because I don't think it very likely that one can get interested in derivative junk and not one day wonder what it was derived from. But, as has been so often mentioned in the text, much of the ground from 1830 – more especially from 1880 – is still inadequately charted. The great lack is in illustrations, from photographs and drawings – so one has had to browse about in periodicals and in manufacturers' records to inform one's browsing in the shops.

On general collecting, then, it might be profitable to start with M. Lambert and Enid Marx's delightful and most informative work *English Popular Art* (Batsford, 1951) which covers many of the items we have looked at – and much else besides, things you can't collect but can go and look at, like weather vanes and pargetting. In *High Victorian Design* (Architectural Press, 1951) Dr Nikolaus Penzner looks at the exhibits of 1851 with learning, judgment and humour: and *A Nineteenth-century Miscellany*, a booklet from the Harris Museum, Preston, sheds light in some dark corners. The fine *Connoisseur Period Guides* (The Connoisseur) have produced a volume, *Early Victorian* 1830–1860, which brings the story in all departments down to that date, while *Regency*

Antiques (Batsford, 1953) by Brian Reade examines with learning and also taste many things of his period which even we can aspire to.

That untiring team, Mr G. Bernard Hughes and Mrs Therle Hughes, continue to produce volume after volume in which, while leaving the reader to form his own aesthetic judgments, they give him an immense amount of information about an immense number of things, especially about manufacturing processes, which many antiquarians tend to skip over. If much of their work deals with rarities, they are nevertheless always pushing forward into our 'dark ages' and lighting the way for browsers like you and me. Their more general titles, by one or other or both, are: *After the Regency:* a Guide to late Georgian and Early Victorian Collecting 1820–1860 (Lutterworth Press, 1956); *Collecting Antiques* (Country Life, 1949); *More About Collecting Antiques* (Country Life, 1952); *Horse Brasses and other Small Items for the Collector* (Country Life, 1956); *Small Decorative Antiques* (Lutterworth Press, 1959).

Other useful sources of general information are tradesmen's catalogues, especially those issued by the big stores: I have one of Harrod's for the year 1902 which is a mine of information. Look out, too, for the big volumes of the old *Art Journal*, published from about 1849 onwards. These can usually be picked up for five shillings apiece, and contain series on 'art manufactures' of the day.

You will also do well to hunt the bookshops for old copies of such journals as *Country Life*, *Apollo*, the *Antiques Dealer and Collector*, and others no longer in print.

If you want to try your hand at repairing or refurbishing damaged items, try *The Art and Antique*

Restorer's Handbook, by George Savage (Rockliff, 1954) which tells you about materials and processes.

Some of the books mentioned both above and below will be out of print, and obtainable only at second hand, sometimes at high prices. You can usually tell this by the date, but in any case booksellers will always tell you what is still in print, and at what price. Needless to say, most of these works contain bibliographies which provide further reading lists in specialist fields.

Furniture

There is an immense library of books on furniture, of course, many of them very expensive. But the early periods are well, and very inexpensively, covered in a Pelican by Ralph Fastnedge, *English Furniture Styles from* 1500 *to* 1830 (Penguin Books, 1955); while an admirable summary, with very clear drawings, is given in Barbara Jones's *English Furniture at a Glance* (Architectural Press, 1954), and in pictures by that most readable writer Frank Davis in *A Picture History of Furniture* (Edward Hulton, 1958). From another un-put-down-able writer on antiques, Mr F. Gordon Roe, come three books which are particularly helpful on later work, *English Cottage Furniture*, *Victorian Furniture*, and *Windsor Chairs* (all Phoenix House, 1950–1953).

Glass

Pelican is again in the field here with *Glass Through the Ages*, by E. Barrington Haynes (Penguin Books, 1948), and so too is G. Bernard Hughes with *English Glass for the Collector*, 1660–1860 (Lutterworth, 1958); Mr E. M. Elville offers an admirable balance of technique and appreciation in *English Table Glass*,

English and Irish Cut Glass, and *Paperweights and other Glass Curiosities* (Country Life, 1951–54).

Mr W. A. Thorpe's books, like *English Glass* (with a list of museum collections) and *A History of English and Irish Glass,* are on the level of Mr Honey's, who also, as it happens, turns up with a catalogue of the Victoria and Albert Museum's collection which is now out of print but ought not to be: if anyone has a spare copy I know of at least one quarter in which it would be appreciated.

For specialist fields there is *Milk Glass,* by E. M. Belknap (Crown Publishers, New York, 1949) which is mainly about American items, but has some useful pictures of our SLAGWARE. The same applies to *Victorian Glass,* by Ruth Webb Lee (Framingham Centre, Mass.).

Sealed Bottles by Sheelah Ruggles-Brise (Country Life, 1949) describes its field. Those who are interested in coloured and other fancy glass from Stourbridge might seek out a recently published biography of *John Northwood,* the famous glassmaker and designer, by his son John Northwood, Jun. (Mark and Moody Ltd., Stourbridge, Worcs., 1958). But publishers have so far grossly neglected this field.

Metal

Many are the books on silver, and as usual there is a Pelican to hand in *Silver,* by Gerald Taylor (Penguin Books, 1956); while the Hugheses are about again too with *Three Centuries of English Domestic Silver* (Lutterworth) and, I believe, a recent book on small silver items. *Chats on Old Copper and Brass,* by F. W. Burgess (Benn, revised 1954), and *Chats on Old Pewter,* by H. J. L. Massé (Benn, revised 1950), are old friends in the field, a newcomer being *Antique Pewter of the British Isles*, by Ronald F. Michaelis (Bell, 1955).

The story of *Old Sheffield Plate* (and also Britannia metal) is told most readably by Edward Wenham (Batsford, 1955), and *English Cutlery* is another of the Victoria and Albert Museum's useful illustrated booklets. Although metals are covered in the GENERAL titles already given, there is still a great deal of room for more publishing, especially in Victorian cast-iron and other metalwork, of ever-growing interest to this generation.

Pottery and Porcelain

If you have the courage to start at what seems to be the quite fantastically wrong end of the tunnel, may I diffidently suggest that you get your eye in on pots and potters with the late Mr W. B. Honey? Mr Honey was not only a world-renowned expert, but a man of exquisite taste and sensibility. The fact that he studied mainly the earlier wares, and disliked most of the stuff which we are looking at in the junk shops today is really beside the point, for the standards of judgment he offered in his own field can just as easily be applied to ours. In fact his introduction to Mr Geoffrey Bemrose's *Nineteenth-century English Pottery and Porcelain* (Faber and Faber, 1952) points out that during this era 'in spite of unfavourable conditions the native genius of the English potters did succeed in producing wares which are both beautiful and of permanent value; and it is a task worth while to discover them in the welter of *parvenu* vulgarity that marked the period after the Napoleonic wars . . .' So read Mr Honey's *The Art of the Potter* (Faber and Faber, 1946) for a marvellous set of juxtapositions of pots from the Bronze Age to modern Wedgwood, in itself an education in appreciation; read also his *Old English Porcelain* (Faber and Faber, 1928), the classic work on the eighteenth-century productions; his *English Pottery and Porcelain* (A. & C. Black, 1949); and the many other titles he wrote or edited in the Faber Monographs on Pottery and Porcelain, which now total over thirty and comprise a complete library on ceramics of every country. If you get seriously interested in Chinese pots, then there is his monumental *Ceramic Art of China and other Countries of the Far East* (Faber and Faber, 1945). Mr J. F. Blacker's *Chats on Oriental China* (T. Fisher Unwin, 1911) can often be found secondhand.

Those interested in STAFFORDSHIRE PRINTED EARTHENWARE will find some useful material on American (and English) views in *The Old China Book*, by N. Hudson Moore (New York, 1903). The Spode contribution to this field is covered with a wealth of pattern illustrations by Sydney B. Williams in *Antique Blue and White Spode*.

Pottery generally is written about both authoritatively and readably by Mr Reginald G. Haggar in *English Country Pottery* and *Staffordshire Chimney Ornaments* (Phoenix House, 1950 and 1955 respectively); *English Pottery Figures*, 1660–1860, and *Recent Ceramic Sculpture* (Tiranti, 1947 and 1946 respectively). Mr Haggar teams up with Wolf Mankowitz in *The Concise Encyclopedia of English Pottery and Porcelain* (Andre Deutsch, 1957) which is exactly what it claims to be and comes bang up to the present. Mr G. Bernard Hughes (whose 'general' books should also be looked at for chapters on ceramic matters) has pushed farther forward than anyone else in *Victorian Pottery and Porcelain* (Lutterworth, 1959) in, as usual, immense detail; while an admirable collection of photographs, with short summary histories, showing items from mediaeval jugs to modern acid jars, is to be found in Griselda Lewis's *English Pottery* (Hulton Press, 1956). Two Pelicans by George Savage, *Pottery Through the Ages*, and *Porcelain Through the Ages* (Penguin Books 1959 and 1954 respectively) give the world picture with authority and judgment in the cheapest possible form. For a near-contemporary view of Victorian pottery, and most exhaustive detail about the pottery firms themselves, try to find a copy of *Nineteenth-century English Ceramic Art*, by J. F. Blacker (Stanley Paul, 1911). A recent book on this era is *Victorian Pottery*, by Hugh Wakefield (Herbert Jenkins, 1962).

Books on Marks are dealt with under that head.

Mocha Pottery is covered in a pamphlet by N. Teulon-Porter, published by the City of Stoke-on-Trent Museum and Art Gallery, who are also responsible for Mr G. J. V. Bemrose's guide to the Collection of English Lustre Ware. The whole story of potlids is covered in *The Potlid Recorder*, by H. G. Clarke, 1950.

Oddments

On particular subjects we may cite *Victorian Jewellery*, by Margaret Flower (Cassell, 1951), as well as *English Victorian Jewellery*, by Ernle Bradford (Country Life, 1959); *The English Print*, by Basil Gray (Benn, 1937); *Fine Prints*, by Frederick Wedmore (Grant, 1910); *Old Clocks for Modern Use*, by Edward Wenham (Bell); *The Book of the Wine Label*, by Dr N. M. Penzer (1949), also covering cordial, sauce, perfume and other labels; and *English Dolls, Effigies and Puppets*, by Alice K. Early (Batsford, 1955). I am told, though I have not seen them, that *Snuff and Snuff Boxes*, by H. McCausland (1951), *Old English Barometers*, by

G. G. and E. F. Bell (1952), *English Vinaigrettes*, by Eileen Ellenbogen (1957), and *The Romance of Lace*, by E. Jones (1951), are all reliable in their field.

Marks and Patterns

Pottery and Porcelain. Nobody interested in pottery of any sort can resist turning a piece bottom up to see if there is a mark. It can, of course, be a most helpful way of identifying its maker and date. But marks can also be a trap. The Chinese, for example, when reproducing an admired piece from the past, will faithfully add its mark, not with any intention of deceiving, but simply from respect for a distinguished predecessor.

Later potters have done the same thing – with less worthy motives. So we find such highly esteemed factories as CHELSEA using the MEISSEN mark, WORCESTER passing itself off as CHELSEA, MINTONS flying the banner of SÈVRES, and almost everybody at some stage or other making up some sort of device which they hoped would be taken for Chinese. Some potters still working today have even imitated their own earlier marks, and if that isn't forgery it certainly doesn't make life any easier for the collector.

So the golden rule with marks is to use them, but not to be used by them. In other words, make sure first of everything else – paste, style, quality of potting, glaze and those highly subtle things 'feel' and 'look'. If the mark is right as well, then the piece is, as they say in the trade, *right*.

The marks on the following pages are only a tiny proportion of those which have been recorded and collected. Many of the books in the READING LIST give useful selections, but there are also a number of books entirely devoted to marks. *The Pocket Book of*

English Ceramic Marks (and those of Wales, Scotland and Ireland), by J. P. Cushion (Faber and Faber, 1954), is a modestly priced one, and foreign marks are also given in the *Handbook of Pottery and Porcelain Marks* (Faber and Faber, 1956) in which the same author collaborated with his late colleague at the Victoria and Albert Museum, Mr W. B. Honey, and covered the marks of other countries as well. One I have found very useful, which although from America contains a surprising number of English marks, is the *Handbook of Old Pottery and Porcelain Marks*, by C. Jordan Thorn (Tudor Publishing Company, New York, 1947).

Most of what you want to know about Chinese marks is in *Chinese Marks and Symbols*, published by *The Antique Collector*, a tiny booklet which really does fit into the waistcoat pocket.

Registry Marks. A mark often found, not only on pottery and porcelain, but also on articles in other materials, was the 'diamond' showing the date a design was registered at the Patent Office. These records have now been transferred to the Public Record Office, who have loaned them temporarily to the Victoria and Albert Museum, South Kensington, London, S.W.7. Tables (given in *More Looking in Junk Shops*) will enable you to work out the date a design was registered, but to learn the makers' name you must apply to the Museum.

Silver and Sheffield Plate Marks. A handy pocket guide to these is given in a small booklet obtainable from most silversmiths for 7s., with the resounding title of *British and Irish Silver Assay Office Marks 1544–1954, with Notes on Gold Markings, and Marks on Foreign Imported Silver and Gold Plate. Also Old Sheffield Plate Makers' Marks*, by Frederick Bradbury (J. W. Northend, Sheffield).

SOME SPECIMEN POTTERY AND PORCELAIN MARKS

    Wm. Adams & Sons

B. W. M. & CO.   Brown Westhead, Moore & Co.

   W. Brownfield & Sons

S   Salopian   Caughley

   Chelsea

Coalport   Coalport

   W. T. Copeland & Sons

   Copeland & Garrett, Stoke

   Davenport, Longport

   Derby

   Dunn, Bennett & Co., Hanley

Some Specimen Pottery and Porcelain Marks

 W. H. Goss, Stoke

 Leeds

MEIGH Charles Meigh & Sons, Hanley

J. M. & S. Job Meigh & Sons, Hanley

 Mintons Ltd., Stoke

  Minton & Boyle, Stoke

MASON'S PATENT IRONSTONE CHINA

C. J. Mason

New Hall, Shelton

'F. & R. Pratt' F. & R. Pratt, Fenton

J.W.R.
Stone China J. & W. Ridgeway, Hanley

Some Specimen Pottery and Porcelain Marks

W. R. & CO.
                    Wm. Ridgeway & Co., Hanley

ROCKINGHAM

Rockingham Works
Brameld

                    Rockingham

S. S. LTD.
LONGTON
                    Sampson Smith Ltd., Longton

SPODE
Felspar Porcelain
                    Josiah Spode

R. S. W.
                    R. Steveson & Williams, Cobridge

WEDGWOOD
                    Wedgwood

                    Worcester

BFB

Chamberlain
Worcester

George Grainger
Royal China Works
Worcester